Amanda, Perfectly Made

Amanda, Perfectly Made

A Caregiver's Journey

Laurel Rausch Greshel

SEPT. 2013

To: Congresswoman Beutler
    With love and best wishes
to Abigail Rose and her family...
all the way from Detroit!

♡ Laurel

iUniverse, Inc.
Bloomington

Amanda, Perfectly Made
A Caregiver's Journey

All Bible verses are quoted from the New International Version.

iUniverse books may be ordered through booksellers or by contacting:

iUniverse
1663 Liberty Drive
Bloomington, IN 47403
www.iuniverse.com
1-800-Authors (1-800-288-4677)

ISBN: 978-1-4759-4921-6 (sc)
ISBN: 978-1-4759-4923-0 (e)
ISBN: 978-1-4759-4922-3 (dj)

Library of Congress Control Number: 2012916749

Printed in the United States of America

iUniverse rev. date: 9/26/2012

Contents

Introduction

After twenty-nine years of experience raising a handicapped daughter, it was time to tell her story. Amanda was born with spina bifida, and there were no parenting books to explain how to handle the surgeries, challenges, emotional issues, loneliness, anger, sadness, and frustrations of caring for a handicapped daughter. If only someone would have stepped in to help. Merely phrases like "I know how you feel" or "I've been there" would have made things easier. Reality can be stressful, shocking, and surprising. According to the *National Alliance for Caregiving,* "more than 65 million people—29% of the U.S. population—provide care to a family member." While this statistic includes care to both young and elderly family members, reality demonstrates one in thirty-three babies are born each year with some kind of birth defect.

This story of Amanda's upbringing could not have been told without including the spiritual experiences of the journey. As Amanda's parent and caregiver, enduring the sometimes very difficult years was possible only through strength and faith from a relationship with God. Challenges abounded and easily threatened the stability of family, marriage, and even personal sanity. Since there were others out there in a similar setting, God's guiding hand inspired the writing of this story. With statistics showing that there are millions of caregivers out there, this story is for you, because "I know how you feel."

By sharing the many intimate challenges faced by Amanda's mom through the years, you will hopefully gain understanding of how to handle your own caregiver situations. Whether you are personally a parent or caregiver, or whether you are a friend or professional who deals with a special-needs population, you will find bits of helpful advice and insights sprinkled throughout the book. These bits of advice or helpful hints have been singled out as sidebar notes titled "The Helping Hand." Snippets of interesting information or various facts have also been singled out for you as a "Pass It On" note. Since this story is one driven by faith, personal lessons learned from God have been titled in a sidebar as "Whispers from God." As the story unfolds with painful honesty and intimate detail, perhaps you will be able to relate and find both answer and inspiration.

Amanda, Perfectly Made should truly be read in its entirety. The story is indeed a journey to be traveled from start to finish, as emotions and needs changed and this full-time mom became a full-time caregiver. If you are a friend or professional who has a relationship with someone who is caregiver to a child or adult, you may find it helpful to search the chapters for specific areas of interest, such as "Should Amanda Have a Sister?" or "Please Listen to the Patient's Parents!" It is humbling to have you reading this story of Amanda, but even more, it is healing for the painful challenges we have faced through the years if by reading it, you may find an answer, some understanding, a solution, empathy, or peace from our experience.

1
The Life-Changing Phone Call

Monday morning August 1, 1983, was when our whole world changed. My husband, Ted, had already started his day several hours ahead of me. As a salesman with a multistate sales territory, he had left before the sun was even up to make the long drive to Indiana. I had quit my job several weeks earlier and, at two weeks shy of being nine months pregnant with our first child, enjoyed the luxury of sleeping in and moving at a slower pace.

At just after nine o'clock in the morning, my phone rang. It was my doctor. In a very anxious and concerned voice, he tried to explain the findings of my ultrasound, which had been done on Friday, just before the weekend. It had been my one and only ultrasound, as these were the early eighties—before ultrasounds were done so often and routinely for pregnant mothers. I felt as though all the air had been sucked out of the room as I struggled to understand what he was telling me. Words, as if playing off a teleprompter, drifted by in slow motion: "very little brain ... very serious ... you must see a specialist in Detroit … I don't know if you'll be bringing a baby home or not … appointment tomorrow …"

I cannot explain how I felt. It was like a waterfall of bad news had just poured all over me. I felt like I was suddenly drowning. A feeling of panic washed over me as I desperately tried to keep my head above water. As I tried to grasp the news from the doctor, I felt as though I was treading in deep, turbulent water. Everything became thick and slow, and I had such a suffocating feeling of desperation. I knew I needed to reach Ted right away, but these were the days before he or most anyone had a pager or a cell phone. I called the local office that he worked from and somehow made enough sense to the office manager, Margie. She said she would get a message through to Ted.

Margie was able to determine where Ted was making his sales call and connected with a receptionist there. Ted had pretty much just arrived and was immediately told he had an important call. Margie gave him the scattered details that she had gathered from me. Ted was also swept away by this flood of life-changing news and literally collapsed to his knees in front of the receptionist's desk. I believe he made a call to me, we had a confused exchange of information, and he got back in his car to make the long drive home.

WHISPERS FROM GOD

Jeremiah 29:11a *For I know the plans I have for you, declares the Lord.*

The remainder of the day was a blur. I am not sure who I called or what we talked about. I waited alone through the long hours until Ted returned home. I can only recall an afternoon of tears and talks on the phone. How we even slept that night, I don't know, but the next day was to take us to Detroit and a specialist.

2
First Comes Love, Then Comes Marriage: What Is Spina Bifida Anyway?

I've heard it said that "beginning is halfway to done." It has been many months, if not years, that I have struggled with starting this book. God has been patiently tapping me on the shoulder to start writing, and the tapping seemed to be occurring more often lately and with a little sprinkling of urgency. Fear has been my biggest challenge in starting. Not just the fear of trying to do something that I have never done before (actually write a book), but the simple fact that to begin something suggests an end. And since this book is about the life of my daughter Amanda, the end of this book suggests *her* end. Sickness comes more easily and premature death is more likely for handicapped children or anyone else challenged by serious health issues. So I am frightened at how this book may end, but am driven by personal passion and God's patient encouragement. So, this is the story of Amanda Lynn Greshel, and how she has shaped my life and the lives of family and friends around me.

In telling the story of the life of a person, I think it only fitting to give at least a brief background of the people involved in that story. My name is Laurel, and in 1977 I went away to Ashland College in Ashland, Ohio, because that's what you did after graduating from high school. You went to college. I was pretty smart and even got a scholarship. I had no clue as to what I was going to study, but hoped I would figure that out sometime in the next four college years. Having just gotten over a broken heart in a high-school relationship, I had set my mind on going to college and making as many new girlfriends as I could.

Two weeks after arriving on campus, I met Ted. I fell for him and fell hard. I know for sure now that it was one of those meant-to-be things. God's plan was for Ted and me to meet. Ted was, is, and continues to be my best friend, soul mate, partner, support, companion, lover, and husband till death do us part. Ted was a senior, and I couldn't believe with his blond hair, sparkling blue-gray eyes, and pleasant, witty personality, that no girl had yet snatched him up! Hardly a day went by after our meeting that we weren't together. We finished that year of school together, and by the next year's Christmas we were engaged. After almost two years to the day of our meeting, we were married.

I believe it is significant to know that Amanda grew up with two parents who were very much in love and committed to each other. That was a definite advantage to her, as it would be to any child in a family. It was good for Ted and me as well.

As with most couples who have been married for a time, we reached a stage where we were ready to start our family. By this time, we had been married about three years. We had worked, saved, and purchased our first house. We were ready to expand. Being a sometimes impatient person, I got angry when I didn't get pregnant right away. The anger quickly turned to irrational anxiety as I anguished over why I wasn't getting pregnant. We were ready for a baby and I wanted it now; I didn't want any problems or delays in getting what I wanted! I'm sure many of you who have dealt with infertility can relate to the tears shed at each passing month. But the doctor said to give it a year of trying before starting any kind of infertility treatment.

Before that year was up, we were expecting! The pregnancy-test results confirmed I was pregnant, but I still found it surreal and hard to believe. I felt the same. My stomach was still flat. Was there really, truly, a little person growing inside of me? What would he or she look like? What would life be like with a baby added to our household? Would it be a he or a she? Typical questions, I'm sure, of most expecting couples. Since Ted was the only son of an only son, we were really hoping for a boy to carry on the family name. In hindsight, that was really of little importance to worry about. There wasn't a kingdom or a family business that was doomed to inexistence should we not produce a male heir. I think what God ended up giving us was far better.

For the most part, my pregnancy was fairly easy except for one little scare. Sometime in my first trimester, I started spotting. Having agonized over getting pregnant and now having a threat like this that might be the start of a premature end, I absolutely panicked. I called the doctor's office and was told by the sweet, hushed, voice of the doctor's assistant that sometimes "these things happen, and we have to let nature take its course." I didn't think that was much help at all, and I remember distinctly driving home from work after that little phone conversation and pleading to God to stop the bleeding. With tears in my eyes, I begged for this pregnancy to hold and pledged that I would welcome any baby God gave me.

When I learned later that my daughter's birth defect occurs in the first three to four weeks of pregnancy and that many times those embryos naturally abort because the body just senses that "something is wrong," I wondered, if I had not prayed so desperately, was that pregnancy originally doomed to failure? Was my body trying to get rid of something gone wrong? Did God hear my plea and rescue this pregnancy? This whole little dramatic

---
WHISPERS FROM GOD

Psalm 139:13 *For you created my inmost being; you knit me together in my mother's womb.*

scenario lasted maybe twenty-four hours, as the bleeding stopped within hours. I probably would have forgotten the whole incident—except Amanda *was* born with something wrong. As wrong and as mean as this sounds, there have been some challenging times with Amanda when I've remembered this short episode and reminded myself that one has to be careful what one prays for.

The remainder of my pregnancy was normal: a little bit of nausea at the beginning, typical cravings, and a normal weight gain for me. Keep in mind that this was 1983, and fetal ultrasounds were not routine. If an ultrasound would have been done early on like they do today, her birth defect would have been discovered right away. Fetal surgery, which is surgery performed on a baby still inside its mom, might have helped a lot. But my baby always had a strong, steady heartbeat, and I always felt her moving. After her delivery, I was asked countless times if I had sensed anything wrong or if I had worried that she didn't kick enough. Since it was my first pregnancy, those were challenging questions to answer, if not downright silly ones, as I had no other experiences to compare to! Everything felt just fine and normal to me all along. Because Amanda's birth defect includes paralysis, the doctors thought that perhaps I should have noticed that I wasn't kicked quite as much as "normal." Well, she moved all right, and must have made up for her lack of leg movement by keeping her arms swinging!

We were down to the last two weeks before my due date. At my checkup visit with my doctor, he must have sensed something. In fact, I remember his exact words were that "there's nothing scientific that I can put my finger on, but let's have a few tests to be sure everything is all right." Well, that was enough to get any pregnant mom's heart beating faster! It was sometime midweek, and he scheduled a stress test and an ultrasound for Friday.

Both tests were done Friday morning, and they went quite smoothly as far as I could tell. The technician who did my ultrasound was a man I knew from church. He was very quiet during the whole thing, but he was a quiet man in general so I thought little of it. I remember I asked him about what he saw, and he pointed at some gray image on the screen and said that it was some part of my baby. I don't really remember. Some twenty years later, I ran into him at the same hospital and finally spoke to him about how hard it must have been to see such a damaged baby, but not be able to say anything about it. It is up to the doctor to reveal any diagnosis or results, and it was this technician's job to do the test. My church friend still had a vivid memory of my scan and confirmed to me how difficult it was to say nothing.

I went home from my tests and heard nothing from my doctor all afternoon. Surely, if something were wrong, he would have called immediately. My brother and his wife came to visit from out of state for the weekend, and quite frankly, the tests and all associated anxiety were forgotten. No news is good news, right?

Monday we got the news, and that's when our world changed. Funny how we are always reminded to count our blessings and to give thanks for what we have, because life can change in the blink of an eye. Yet, most of us give our little patronizing prayers of thanks with subliminal greedy desires for all the

---
PASS IT ON

Spina bifida occurs in seven out of every 10,000 births in the United States.

---

additional blessings that would make life even better, not ever expecting to be one of those unfortunates who actually get dealt that life-changing event. For Ted and me, life was going just as planned. We had spent a lovely weekend with visiting family. Ted had a good job, and we lived comfortably in our home, which we had been fixing up since purchasing it two years earlier. Like a beautiful quilt being pieced together with fabrics that were chosen by both Ted and me, we had picked the pattern we wanted as we worked together constructing our lives together. We had created the perfect baby nursery with fresh wallpaper, waiting for us to bring home the perfect baby. The life we were planning, like a quilt, was starting to take shape when the fabric and design were suddenly changed on us. My Monday phone call from the doctor changed our design completely. As I waited for Ted to drive home from Indiana, we both felt our plans unraveling. The road had turned, plans had changed, and the previous design disintegrated before our eyes like fraying fabric.

Tuesday morning, Ted and I drove the twenty-five minutes to Hutzel Hospital in Detroit. Our home, friends, church, jobs, and frequented stores were all in our friendly and familiar suburban life that was twenty-three miles from the city of Detroit. To us, a trip to Detroit was like journeying to a foreign land. We were to see Dr. Marin, an ob/gyn who was a specialist. Funny that I don't remember what he specialized in, but I think it was high-risk pregnancies. Dr. Marin was a very kind man, who was soft spoken, of medium build, with dark hair, who got right down to business. The first step was a repeat of an ultrasound of my baby, which confirmed the previous abnormal findings. Apparently there was a great accumulation of fluid in her head, which was pressing on and compressing her brain. The technical term is hydrocephalus. The doctor was, however, quite confident that my baby also had spina bifida, and I remember him moving the scanner back and forth, over and over again, on my belly to try and prove what he wanted to see on her spine. He never got his clear picture. Next, he decided an amniocentesis would be helpful. An amniocentesis involves using a very long needle to withdraw some amniotic fluid from around the baby. Much can be determined from this fluid about a baby's health. Let me tell you, that needle was huge; and in the stressed-out, scared state that I was in, it hurt much worse than it's supposed to. Especially in late pregnancy, when amniotic fluid levels are greatly decreased, and a sampling took numerous pokes to get it right and to find a pocket of fluid to draw from. Throughout all the testing and stressful long day of unanswered questions, all I kept thinking was, "Get this baby out of me and start helping it."

Our parting conversation with Dr. Marin basically confirmed that our baby definitely had hydrocephalus and, most likely, spina bifida. He might as well have been speaking another language to us, as these were terms we had never heard of before. We listened to splashes of explanation from Dr. Marin about these foreign conditions that had afflicted our baby. In our naïveté and shock, we had no concept of the great medical issues we were facing; we tried to ignore the bad and focus on the healthy baby we were expecting. Okay, so maybe we might have to see our baby through a couple of fix-it surgeries, but we were still counting on the happily-ever-after. The final big question for us was to decide whether we wanted to continue to full term and deliver when I went into labor or to do a C-section right away and start treatment. There was no question for us. We already understood that a vaginal delivery could be traumatic for a baby whose head was already under pressure from extreme hydrocephalus. We also felt that we needed to find out exactly what we were dealing with to start helping our baby. At this point, we decided to continue under the medical care of Dr. Marin. He was, after all, a specialist in a big-city hospital. There was also the benefit of the Children's Hospital of Michigan being conveniently located down the street. Ted and I went home to try and rest. My C-section was scheduled for the next day.

To help you understand much of what happened next, I think it best to share with you a little medical background in regard to Amanda's birth defects. Amanda has spina bifida. With spina bifida, something happens during the spinal cord development. The vertebrae in our backs are hollow, with all the fragile nerves running through the core. The bony, hard vertebrae serve as both protection and container for all the long spaghetti-like strands of nerves from brain to tailbone. With spina bifida, one of those vertebrae fails to close completely into its tubular shape, and, of course, the nerves from defect on down kind of go "splat." They get broken and tangled, and as with any neck or spinal injury, the higher the "break," the higher the level of paralysis. A broken neck can make a person a quadriplegic. A back that is broken further down on the spine may result only in paraplegia. The same holds true for a spina bifida defect: the higher up the damaged vertebrae is, the higher up the paralysis on a person's body.

Because Dr. Marin could not visualize on ultrasound where Amanda's spina bifida defect was—or if it was even present, we had no idea whatsoever the amount of paralysis our baby might have. Sometimes, there is a protruding sack of membrane and nerves coming out of the defect in the back as well, and this is what Dr. Marin was trying to visualize with his persistent ultrasound scanning. Occasionally spina bifida defects are hidden under the skin, but more commonly the defect presents itself as either an open hole or sore, with even some nerves and tissue spilling out. To get the true picture, we would have to wait until our baby was born.

In addition to the back defect, most spina bifida patients also have hydrocephalus. This is more commonly known as "water on the brain." Our bodies are remarkable in all their functions, including the way they continually produce fluid to surround our brains and spinal cords. For some reason, in spina bifida patients, the mechanism for draining off the extra fluid as it continually replenishes

THE HELPING HAND

After parents receive an unfavorable medical diagnosis for their child, the emotional ride can be painfully confusing. As friend or family to the parents, you can show support by letting them know you are thinking of them and are available when they need you.

11

itself is broken. The body produces the fluid, but it gets trapped and cannot drain. The technician who first did my ultrasound saw a picture of a baby with a head filled up with fluid, and a brain compressed tightly against the inside of her skull. There was more fluid than brain. That's what the doctor meant when he told me that my baby didn't have much of a brain. The "water on the brain" then strongly suggested spina bifida, as they usually go hand in hand.

Ted and I came home that Tuesday from our long hospital day in Detroit emotionally drained. Neither of us had family close by, so the phone calls became fatiguing—both from them and our circle of church-family friends in the area. We also came home hungry and decided that a dinner out at the local Chinese restaurant would get us away from the house phone and feed our hungry bodies as well. When we got to the restaurant, the pastor of our church was already dining there with his wife and a doctor who was a member of our congregation. I remember exchanging some conversation with them, but they pretty much left us alone. Ted and I learned later that they had actually gone out to dinner to discuss *us*! I guess we were suddenly quite a phenomenon, as we were the first family at our church to experience having such a medically challenged baby.

Looking back, I see this as purely an example of how our dear church family sought for understanding of a medical challenge that we were facing and how it would affect our lives and how they could help us. Our church family was also praying for us at this time. I am sure it was their prayers that held us together. I can't say that we were panicked or hysterical with fear at this point. I can only remember a "numb peace."

3
Not Your Usual Newborn:
Reactions to the Bad News

August 3, 1983, was delivery day. It was just Ted and me who traveled, again, to the hospital in Detroit for my scheduled C-section. Even though the drive was a reasonable half-hour journey, it was uncomfortable leaving our community to go to a city of unknowns. It was like we were the condemned, making our walk to the gallows. Although I know we were breathing, it was as if we were holding our breaths in anticipation of what our baby was going to look like. With all the medical talk about hydrocephalus and spina bifida, we were almost expecting some sort of monster baby.

As I was being prepped for the surgery, I remember being scared about all that was being done to me by the nurses. No one had talked to me about what to expect during a C-section. The hospital staff and nurses were all very kind to me but a bit restrained, as if they were afraid to say anything that would refer to the monster baby I was about to deliver. Ted was not with me during all the prep work. While the nurses were starting IVs and getting me situated in the operating room,

Ted was changing into operating room-approved daddy garb. The many minutes we were temporarily apart felt more like hours to me; I remember just wanting him there. I needed someone familiar, who loved me and was on my team, with this impending and frightening challenge.

When everything was ready, Ted was allowed in, although I didn't recognize him at first behind all the hospital garb and mask they made him wear. But I had my Ted with me. I recall the C-section being quite unpleasant, as they had trouble getting me all the way numb and I could feel a lot of the cutting and tugging. As they grabbed my baby and pulled her out of me, I felt as though my insides were being sucked inside out. But then, I heard her cry. A newborn baby cry! It didn't sound like any monster sound. And there weren't all kinds of alarms and panicked voices calling for a crash cart, because our little baby was holding her own and breathing with a heart that was beating just fine on its own. I heard Ted whisper to me "it's a girl," and I remember asking to see her. In my foggy, drugged state, I remember seeing a normal little pink baby, who seemed quite ordinary to me. I then asked to see her back, and the nurse turned her over; I have a very vague memory of a round, red, open sore on her back about the size of a golf ball. They took our Amanda away then, and I received another dose of some IV drugs that put me deeper into a fog, with some recollection of accompanying green puke.

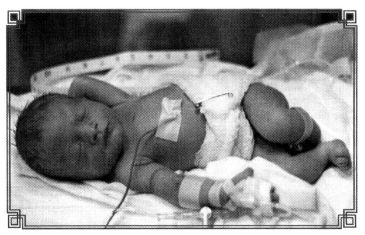

Happy birthday, Amanda Lynn Greshel, August 3, 1983.

It is interesting how people respond to situations that are not usual or normal. When faced with adversity, people will react according to past learned experiences, any knowledge gathered over the years, any peace or strength their faith may offer, as well as personality influences. With sudden, life-changing, out-of-the-ordinary circumstances, the reactions are quite diverse.

In the day or two before Amanda's birth, Ted and I made many phone calls to friends and family to share with them the news of our baby's medical problems and impending birth. Several of those phone calls were to my parents, who, at the time, lived a six-hour drive away in Kentucky. This was to be their first grandchild, so I am sure there was a preconceived vision of that first, healthy, pink, and perfect little baby. I am sure they were devastated as we passed on news to them about the medical problems we were suddenly facing with our baby.

I must pause, now, for another quick medical lesson. With the condition of hydrocephalus, or water on the brain as it is known in layman's terms, the head will continue to swell if there is no way to drain off the extra cerebral spinal fluid. Babies with this condition, in the past, had no hope. Their little heads would swell and swell, while the brain got squished. The brain, under such pressure, could not function normally, and these babies ended up in a vegetative state, with grossly enlarged heads, until they died.

About fifty years ago, a man whose child was stricken with hydrocephalus developed a type of tubing, or "shunt," that could drain off the excess fluid. These shunts are surgically placed and have saved the lives of many babies with hydrocephalus. Although they have had problems with them over the years, the resulting modifications and improvements over time have made them a miracle for those who need them. I need to also add that, even with shunting of the fluid, there are oftentimes various degrees of brain damage, with resulting deficits in intelligence.

So, let's get back to my parents. After hearing from us over the phone about our unborn baby's medical problems, they naturally made phone calls to other family members to share the news. I must point out that, as couples go, my mom was the talker and my dad was the listener. With an outward display of calm, any questions or concerns from Pop always got channeled through Mom. I never really knew what Pop was thinking or feeling, as he took a backseat to Mom, the spokesperson for this couple. I don't recall if it was Monday or Tuesday night before Amanda's birth, but I will never forget what I heard from my mom. As she sobbed to me over the phone, my mother gave the advice, "Don't worry, Laurel. Aunt Martha knew of a family with a baby with water on the brain and it died within a year. You're young, and you can have more children." Even today I cry when I recall those words, although time has softened the sting. To add insult to injury, my aunt's daughter was pregnant at the same time and due within a few weeks. I was informed that my cousin would not be told about my baby because it might upset her and, heaven forbid, if this condition were genetic, her baby might be stricken with the same fate. To put it bluntly, those were not the words of love and encouragement I was expecting from my mom. But over the years, I have come to realize that my mom just did not know how to handle the situation of a multiply handicapped child. I believe, out of love, she was just trying to make all the bad go away.

My mom's difficulty with the whole situation continued to be evident when she and my dad first came to visit me in the hospital after Amanda's birth. Mom's guard was definitely up, as I recollect her with her arms crossed and locked in front of her in the stereotypical pose of defiance. Pop sat quietly on the side. A social worker had stopped by at the same time to share some information about spina bifida children.

THE HELPING HAND

When a newborn presents with a grim diagnosis, the parent does not want to hear the bad news. Natural mothering instincts take over as the parent fights for the survival of his or her newborn. Friends and family need to be supportive and encouraging. Parents need people to be cheerleaders, not grim reapers.

Patient and soft-spoken, the social worker answered our many questions and even had several booklets for us to read. My mom grappled with her own words, as she was trying to get some definitive answers to her questions about what we could expect from Amanda in the future. The social worker played dumb, I realized, as she was trying to get my mom to just come out and come to terms with everything and ask the

17

darned question! *Was Amanda going to be normal or retarded?* I knew that's what my mom was thinking. Of course, it was too early for answers to any kind of questions like that.

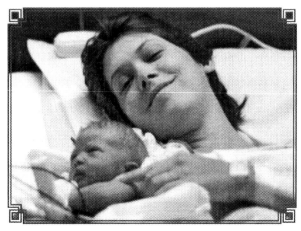

Holding Amanda for the first time.

With the birth of our daughter, Amanda, we were a family now. After an hour or so in the recovery room, I was moved to my hospital room to recover from my C-section. Amanda was in the hospital's newborn nursery, but was to be transferred down the street to the Children's Hospital of Michigan. A transfer team came to get Amanda for the big ride down the street, and Ted asked them if they could please stop by to see me first. He knew how fervently I was wishing for all the bad to go away. I had not seen our baby since delivery, and my empty arms begged to hold her. After they picked up Amanda from the NICU, Ted directed the transfer team to my room and insisted they hand her over to me so we could take that first normal picture of "Mom and newborn." Still groggy from medication and not able to sit up yet due to the spinal I had, I vaguely remember being handed this little pink wrapped bundle—my daughter! She was cute and pink and warm, and seemed quite "normal" to me.

I realize now that this issue of "normal" is one that has followed us, relentlessly and rudely, through the years. As any parent of a child who is handicapped, whether physically or mentally, knows, we didn't exactly get what we ordered! During those nine months of waiting, we all dream and visualize what our new child will look like and what he or she will be like. Because we didn't get a typical, normal kid, we forever are comparing, hoping, looking, wishing, and grasping at anything "normal" we can get. The other issue that has plagued us over the years with Amanda is that of "mourning." Although not a literal death, we have had to say good-bye to the normal, healthy newborn that we did not get. Throughout the years, as the typical milestone moments come around, as we hope for the "normal" and do not get it, we continually get reminded once again that we got something a little different in the shape and form of our dear Amanda. Any sad feelings of loss or disappointment must be buried with the child we didn't get, and an acceptance made of the goals and accomplishments that Amanda herself makes.

Amanda was born on August 3, and as that day ended, we could at least exhale and know that we had all the initial worries of that day behind us. Amanda may have come into this world a little damaged, but she was strong. Naturally, there's always concern for a mom to safely deliver her newborn. Somehow Ted managed to divide his time between two hospitals visiting both his wife and daughter, field all the phone calls from friends and family that were coming through to the phone at home, take care of business at work, and orchestrate visits from both his parents and mine.

Ted's parents offered a different kind of reaction to Amanda's birth. I was still in the hospital recovering from my C-section when Ted's folks came to visit. Amanda had been transferred to the Children's Hospital down the street, and the doctor was allowing me to take a ride down the street once a day to visit her. Dressed in my robe and slippers, I was taken to the front door of the hospital by wheelchair, where Ted's dad was waiting to play chauffeur. As Ted, his parents and I drove the short distance down the street, Ted's dad cheerfully announced, "You guys are so lucky! God gave us just ordinary kids, and you got a special one!" Please know that it was said with complete sincerity. I think I was too stunned to reply; I was at a complete loss for words at this remark. On the inside, I was screaming, "You've got to be kidding!" I could not fathom that my current situation was anything like "lucky," and my father-in-law was obviously a raging lunatic! His comment got filed, for the time being, in the back of my brain. I was too tired and preoccupied to process it at the time. Now with hindsight, I know that Ted's dad and mom are people very strong in their faith and seek God first in all things. Because of them, Amanda was, and always is, the recipient of prayers from many people around the world. In the eyes of Ted's parents, Amanda was simply part of God's plan and a blessing to all, whereby we would learn and grow and come closer in our relationship to God.

The reaction of basically everyone else to Amanda was that of great curiosity. We were quick to snap a few Polaroid pictures to show friends because everyone was expecting some strange, deformed baby. What if the baby *did* look grossly different? What would that person say to us at that awkward moment? Like any proud father of a newborn, Ted carried these photos to share with friends while his two girls were still in the hospital. With intense curiosity mixed with fear, people eagerly gazed at the photos of this cute little pink newborn. The awkward tension of that first photo introduction of our daughter dissolved easily and quickly as the person exhaled in relief at the sight of, simply, a baby.

You may wonder where Ted and I were, emotionally, in these early days revolving around Amanda's birth. We were a team, and we were at war. We knew we wanted this baby, our child,

> **WHISPERS FROM GOD**
>
> Psalm 71:14a *As for me, I will always have hope.*

and we were going to fight for her life. Whatever battles or obstacles we were facing, we would face them together. We never actually sat down and discussed it. We never had to.

With a sick baby to consume my time and energy, I quickly healed from my C-section. My doctor made me stay in the hospital longer than a typical post C-section mother does today, because he wanted me to take a little extra time for my own healing. He probably knew the exhausting road I had ahead with caring for Amanda, and was trying to give my body an extra day or two of rest. Once I got out of the hospital, life revolved around the fight for our baby. After a C-section, part of the healing instructions is not to drive. Every day, therefore, either Ted or a friend would make the twenty-five-minute drive to take me down to the hospital in Detroit. There I would spend the day until Ted showed up at the end of his workday to spend time with Amanda as well, and then together we would drive home.

4
What Is This NICU?
Life in a Foreign Land

The Neonatal Intensive Care Unit, or "NICU" for short, is a world of its own. It is a special unit in the hospital, set aside only for sick and premature babies. There are special nurses and doctors devoted to the care of NICU patients, as well as special equipment. To enter this secluded world also takes special preparation. Every morning, I had to scrub my hands up to my elbows with a nylon bristle brush and nasty, gold-brown soap. I stood in front of this big stainless steel sink and scrubbed until my hands and arms were screaming back at me with fiery-red, raw skin. After rinsing and drying, I donned a lovely light yellow gown over my street clothes. This time-consuming process could be pure agony due to the fact that I simply wanted to see my baby, whom I hadn't seen since the day before. Knowing it was for everyone's good to be so scrubbed and germfree still didn't make the process any

> **PASS IT ON**
>
> *You will hear people talk about the "nick-you." That's hospital talk for the NICU.*

easier as I tried not to hurry through it. And then, once washed and properly robed, I might still be made to wait if the doctors happened to be making rounds at that time.

Like most newborns in the NICU, Amanda started out in an "isolette"—a box-shaped bed with a door on the front. It was made of clear Lucite so you could see through it, and its purpose was to keep the tiny patient in a closed environment, away from germs and breezes, as well as being able to keep the little box warm to help with keeping the baby warm. During the day, I could take Amanda out to hold and feed her, although the nurses monitored her temperature to make sure she was staying warm outside her heated box. It always felt so very strange at the end of the day to have to "put Amanda away" in her little box-bed—like we were putting the milk back in the fridge so it wouldn't spoil by the next day.

The reality was, our baby belonged to the rules and regulations of the NICU world. Being so unfamiliar with and intimidated by IV lines, beeping monitors, abundant medical personnel, scary bandages, and various tubes and wires seemingly everywhere, it was easy to surrender our trust to the rules and staff of the NICU. It was like being in a foreign land. Life revolved around somehow getting your baby to come home to your own, more familiar world.

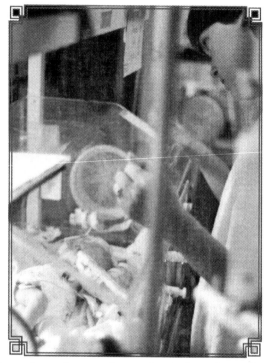

Laurel standing vigil over Amanda in her isolette.

The daily visits to the NICU always began with feelings of fear and anticipation. I naturally walked straight to where I left my baby the night before, and I expected to see her how I last left her. However, things can change overnight. Some mornings, I might find an empty crib, or my baby's crib would be gone! My heartbeat quickened, the panic set in, and I could barely breathe until the nurse told me that my baby was either off having some test done or had been moved to another room. I also took quick stock of the equipment surrounding my baby's crib, because anything new meant a new problem, and things taken away usually meant progress.

I would like to add this paragraph as a "hurrah" and a thank you to the neonatal nurses who took care of our daughter Amanda. Nurses were working in the NICU most likely because they *chose* to work there. Of course, there's always a crabby nurse who might just be having a bad day. But for the most part, the nurses were very caring and compassionate and treated their little patients and the families as if they were their own. I believe they understood, more than most, the daily pain and struggle we parents were going through as we fought for our babies' lives. If we had a bad day with physical setbacks for

---

THE HELPING HAND

The parents of NICU babies regard the nurses as our surrogate family. Regardless of the paycheck they earn for doing their job, we trust them and lean on them for care and love for our children.

Amanda, we would find little notes the next day from the nurses, taped to the isolette. They might say something like, "Thanks, Mom and Dad, for taking such good care of me" or simply "Love you, Mom and Dad." The notes would be signed "from Amanda," as if our own little baby were writing the messages. And the nurses always had a cute little sign with Amanda's name on it taped to her bed, with stickers and pictures. We often left notes back to the nurses, as if from Amanda, thanking them as well for the great care they were giving. So, here's a big "thank you" to all the neonatal nurses out there.

Amanda decked out in NICU attire.

5

Finding Our Way out of the NICU: What's a Shunt?

Life fell into a daily routine for the little Greshel family of three. Daddy would go to work, and Mommy would go to the hospital to be with baby Greshel. That was it. Life had no other purpose at that time. Fortunately, there were no other little Greshels at home to distract us. This is a big issue, however, with many families who have sick ones in the hospital. All interest goes to the sick one in need, and although not deliberately or intentionally, the ones left at home miss out on attention. My heart goes out to siblings of sick children. Please remember that you are loved just as much. Your needs are just not as great as your sick brother's or sister's at this time. Believe me, a mom's heart breaks as she wishes she could create a clone or twin to be in two places at the same time. This would become a great issue for the Greshel family in a couple years. More about that later. Fortunately for Amanda, she had our undivided attention in these early weeks.

Day after day, our visiting routine continued as I learned about Amanda's needs and strived to understand how to take care of her so we could go home and be a family. Besides understanding how shunts work, I had to recognize when they weren't functioning properly. Bandaging the surgical site on Amanda's back was a new skill I was trained to complete. And because Amanda had no feeling or muscle function from about the waist on down, I had to be

> **PASS IT ON**
>
> *Elisabeth Kubler-Ross described the seven stages of grief as shock or disbelief, denial, anger, bargaining, guilt, depression, and acceptance/hope.*

taught how to make sure what was consumed on the top end was coming out in the diaper at the bottom end. In hindsight, it was almost like having Amanda in the "shop" those first weeks: repair and replace a few parts and get all systems running so that we could take home our brand-new, perfect, 1983-model-year Greshel baby! If you are familiar with the seven stages of grief that typify the emotional state of those in mourning, we were certainly in the first couple stages at this time. Shock and denial dominated our emotions, as we felt certain that there really wasn't anything wrong with our daughter that couldn't be fixed. In reality, our hopes, plans, and dreams of having the perfect baby were dead and gone. We just wouldn't believe that this cute little pink baby girl really had all the problems the doctors told us she had.

Every NICU baby has health hurdles to jump. For our Amanda, there were two main health issues. The first was the hole in her back, where her raw spine was exposed. This hole was a literal wick to potentially bring infection directly into her spinal column, which then would take it to her brain. Without surgery or antibiotics, she could have easily died of meningitis—infection of the brain. She had surgery when she was a day old to close that opening. The surgeon had to be rather creative in pulling the skin together, as newborn skin is fairly thin and fragile and there is not any spare skin to work with. The skin on her back was so raw, stretched, and almost burnt-looking that they actually treated it with a daily bandaging and paste of Silvadene, a white cream often used for burned skin. Surgery was successful, although it took many weeks for things to heal. Unlike skin, bones, or muscles, which will heal and grow back together when surgically reconstructed, nerves cannot grow back. The surgery only patches and safely covers and closes the open spine.

Amanda's second hurdle was controlling her hydrocephalus. At the same time that she had surgery to close her back, she had her first shunt put in. To keep Amanda's head from literally blowing up from the collection of cerebral spinal fluid, or CSF, a drainage-type tube had to be surgically inserted. A small hole is drilled in the skull, and a small tube is threaded through the hole into the depths of the brain. The tube snakes out of the hole and runs under the skin, down the neck, across the chest, and finally gets threaded loosely into the abdominal cavity. As fluid

PASS IT ON

In 1956 John W. Holter, a trained mechanic, focused his creative energy and skill with his hands to fashion the first successful shunt valve for hydrocephalus. His invention solved a problem that surgeons had been unable to overcome: helping Holter's son, Casey, overcome the hydrocephalus that accompanied his diagnosis of spina bifida. Mr. Holter's shunt went on to save hundreds of thousands of lives.

builds up in the brain, the pressure causes it to exert force and find "relief" in the top end of the shunt; as in a gutter downspout, the fluid goes into the top end and naturally flows to the bottom end. Excess fluid drains off, where it is absorbed by normal body processes in the abdomen, the brain is not squished, and life is good.

Unfortunately, this is not a perfect world, and shunts can get infected and they can clog up. In newborns, a clogged shunt is easily recognized. Newborns have a "soft spot" on the top of their heads, where the bones of the skull haven't grown all the way together yet. When shunts plug up and fluid on the brain builds up, that soft spot literally gets firm to the touch and actually bulges. Ted and I used to laugh that because we both were constantly touching Amanda's soft spot, she was never going to grow hair there because we were constantly rubbing it off. Besides the bulging soft spot, accumulation of fluid on the brain also makes for a lethargic baby. Several times in that first five and a half weeks during her NICU stay, Amanda's shunt clogged up. Each time resulted in another operation to put in fresh, unclogged parts. Ted and I thought it would be a grand idea if the doctors could engineer a zipper or Velcro opening to facilitate this repetitive surgery to save Amanda's head from all the surgical slices and sutures.

Ted and I grew weary of visiting our daughter every day. All we wanted was to bring her home so we could be a family. The constant daily visits for weeks on end were exhausting. Each day was like a tease, as we were desperate to reach our goal, to obtain that proverbial carrot on the end of the stick, to have our great desire of bringing home our daughter brought a step or two closer. Each day we visited felt like a spin of the roulette wheel, as we hoped and prayed for Lady Luck to be on our side. As each day brought us baby steps closer to our goal, it was not unusual to have a day that brought giant steps backward.

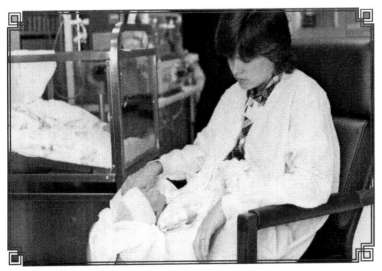

Another day in the NICU.

Unless you've actually had the experience of spending time bedside with a child in the hospital, it's a feeling you'll never understand. Your love for such a child is beyond measure, and since he or she is your own flesh and blood, you feel as though you personally experience everything he or she goes through. Although Amanda had many hurdles to overcome in those early weeks, we at least weren't balancing tediously on a situation of life or death. My heart aches for parents who have newborns who are premature or with damaged hearts or lungs, and for whom life hangs on with such fragility. Ted and I saw many situations like that. Funny how it made us feel lucky. One early life lesson that Ted and I learned was that no matter how bad you think your own situation is, there's always something worse. There's always something to be thankful for—even if it's that your own terrible, horrible situation is not quite as bad as the person's next to you.

As a parent of a struggling newborn, you just want to breathe for your baby, or take the "punches" for your child. You see him or her struggling, and you fight for every breath he or she takes. You feel every needlestick and wish with your whole heart and soul that you could fight the health battles for your child. As I fought with Amanda through every medical challenge, wishing I could bear it all for her, it brought me closer to God in a strange way. So intense is the love of a parent for a child that we would spare him or her from pain and suffering if we could. Every time Amanda has hurt, faced surgery and the painful healing afterward, through all the uncomfortable tests and needlesticks, I would literally crumble to my knees as the tears came fast and hot, and plead with God to spare my child from the pain, to let me take it for her. And then God would whisper to me that He knows how I feel. How horrible was it for God to see His very own son suffer in blood and pain and agony on the cross? How excruciating was God's desire to take away the pain His son was suffering? But He would not, and I could not.

> **THE HELPING HAND**
>
> *To sit vigil at a hospital bedside, while not physically demanding, can leave a parent or caregiver both physically and emotionally exhausted. Hospital fatigue can leave a parent depressed, quick to tears, and slow to understand complicated instructions. Be patient.*

Unless you have had to fight for a sick child or loved one, you just can't imagine the amount of strength it takes and how utterly exhausted you can feel at the end of the day. You may have only sat vigil at the hospital bedside, but every ounce of energy, every beat of your heart, every tear shed or held back, every molecule in your body feels absolutely sucked dry. So you go home and fall, exhausted, into bed to rest and recharge for the next day. Of course, you call the hospital first to talk to the nurse taking care of your baby, to make sure everything is all right, before you can even find sleep.

But, finally, the day came! All systems were "go." Amanda could maintain her own normal body temperature, she was eating well and putting on weight, there was no need for IVs or medications, she was pooping and peeing, and her shunt was working. It was time to take her home. We were terrified! Five and a half weeks of stuff had to be packed up: cards and gifts from friends and families, flowers and plants that still had enough life in them to keep, clothes and blankets we'd brought from home, and lots of hospital stuff, like little bottles of baby formula, bandages for her back, and little hospital-issued bottles of shampoo and baby items like a comb and brush. We dressed Amanda up in a sweet little white dress with pink rosebuds and ribbons on it, and matching bloomers as well. Buckling her securely in her baby carrier, we gathered everything up and were out the door. Ted and I were happy, scared, hesitant, insecure, anxious, and prayerfully hopeful that all would go well. Finally, after five and a half weeks, we were bringing home our baby to be a normal family!

6
Bringing Home the Broken Baby

For most parents who are bringing home their firstborn, life can be pretty scary. All of a sudden there is this new person in the house who can't talk and who didn't come with an instruction book! Is she eating enough? Did I diaper her correctly? Am I burping her enough? Is she too cold? Is she too hot? Why is she crying? There are so many questions and so much to learn! But, like most parents, we figured it out. You learn to "read" your baby—what each cry or sound means, and whether he or she has eaten enough or burped sufficiently.

THE HELPING HAND

Every new mom struggles with knowing how to take care of her baby, even if there are no extraordinary health problems. Moms and babies have been figuring it out for centuries.

Eventually, after days and weeks of trying to figure things out, life falls into its own routine, and you get comfortable with taking care of the baby. Baby feedings, sleep times, and nap times fall into a fairly predictable and familiar pattern, and life takes on a feeling of "normal."

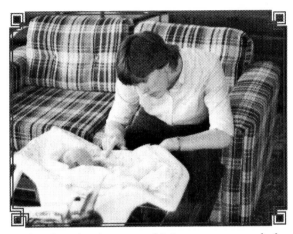

Amanda's first day home, and Mom is concerned already.

Our "normal" wasn't the same as another family's normal, however, as our diaper changes included bandage changes on Amanda's still-healing back. And we were always checking to be sure her shunt was working. Another issue we had that "normal" newborns didn't was Amanda's incontinence. Most people forget that spina bifida is a spinal cord injury. Nerve endings don't connect, and muscles don't work. Muscles control urination and moving your bowels. Dealing with Amanda's incontinence as a baby was a fairly simple task. Babies are diapered and incontinent, anyway, so Amanda wore a diaper like any "normal" baby. When her bladder got overfilled, it spontaneously let go and she'd wet her diaper. Or we could simply push gently on her soft little lower baby belly, and it would push the pee out! For her bowels, we put some lovely chocolate-flavor laxative stuff in her evening bottle, and it produced a poopy diaper every morning.

For the most part, Amanda looked like any usual baby, with her cute diapered bottom, pink little baby outfits, and pink, pudgy baby face. People loved to hold her and play with her, and it was no big deal that she wore a diaper. It was actually not difficult at all to find people to babysit Amanda or even watch her for a night. She was a cute little baby, who wet her diaper, even if you had to push on her cute little baby belly. And little baby Amanda made poopy diapers just like any other pooping little infant. Aside from her shunt and the incontinence issues, Amanda was pretty much your typical baby. There aren't many expectations from a newborn besides eating, sleeping, and diaper changes. We fed and burped her, put her down for naps, gave her rattles to shake, talked to her, and sang her silly songs. I recall the practical advice I received from an experienced NICU nurse who recognized my uneasiness as I anxiously learned to care for my not-so-normal daughter. Her wise words were simply "Take her home and love her."

Two-month-old Amanda at home.

7
When Shunts Go Wrong

As I discussed earlier, Amanda's "soft spot" on her head made it simple to check on whether her shunt was working or not. This soft spot, as its name implies, should be soft. And when it got firm to the touch, or even bulged, it was a red flag that her shunt was not draining like it should and fluid pressure was building up in her head.

Another sign of a shunt not draining was when Amanda would projectile-vomit her feeding. All that pressure on the brain from fluid buildup would result in her puking rather like the stream of water from a fire hose! In our house, it was normal for either Ted or me to lay out a "barf zone" on the opposite side of the couch from where we sat to feed Amanda her bottle. This entailed laying out one of her blankets on the far cushion and arm of the couch or loveseat we were sitting on so that, after feeding Amanda her bottle of formula, we could prop her up on our knee and burp her. We would have her face that other end of the couch, and just in case, if her burping also included shooting barf to the far end of the couch, cleanup was a snap; the blanket would get tossed in the washer, puke all tidily collected in the folds of the blanket.

A third sign we looked for when we were worried about whether her shunt was working was her level of consciousness. If Amanda were sleeping too much and was hard to awaken, that usually meant that CSF had built up and her brain was getting squished. As parents, we would just "know" that she wasn't acting the same—sleepier than usual, not responding with the typical coos or giggles, and her eyes would lose their focus and clarity. She would get this doll-like stare, and sometimes she'd get "sunset eyes," where you would only see the top half of her irises, which looked like setting suns, with the whites of her eyes showing only on the sides and above the "setting" iris. So, if Amanda's soft spot was not soft, her feedings were coming back up to hit the barf zone, or we found that our daughter was just not acting her usual self, we would find ourselves back at Children's Hospital.

It seems like her shunt would plug up every couple of weeks. It was the luck of the draw, I guess. We heard many stories of shunts that lasted for years—and others of shunts that got changed every week. The first time or two were very traumatic to us. Having toiled so hard for so many weeks to bring her to health and home, it was devastating to have to return to the hospital and see our daughter as a patient again. If Amanda slept a little longer than usual or an after-bottle burp seemed more like vomiting than a spit-up, then our parental radar would go up and we would nervously start questioning the patency of her shunt. Was it working? Was it draining? Is she all right? Is her soft spot getting firmer? Is she acting groggy? Should we call the doctor? Should we wait until tomorrow? But the signs of a plugged shunt would eventually become glaringly obvious to us, and once again we would make the drive down to Children's Hospital to see the doctor or, if it were evening or the weekend, we would go to the hospital emergency room. Each time, we were pretty certain that our parental skills of observation and basically our familiarity with our own daughter would result in a diagnosis of a plugged shunt and that surgery was the only way to "unplug" it.

By the time Amanda made it through her first year of life, she had gone through about ten shunt surgeries. The amazing thing about all those shunt surgeries is that they became a "normal" for us. Of course, we were bummed the first time or two it happened. But it is amazing how quickly babies can bounce back after this kind of surgery. We would bring a sleepy, lethargic, bulging-head Amanda into the hospital; they'd put her to sleep in the operating room and take out the clogged parts, put in new parts, stitch her up; and—voilà—she'd wake up and be our happy little baby girl again! It actually became a routine surgery for Amanda, and we'd be in one day and out the next.

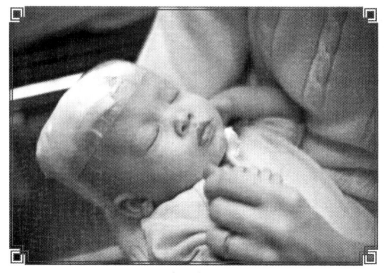

Just another shunt surgery.

The symptoms of a plugged shunt changed as Amanda grew. I already described for you the "head check" where we could tell simply by the firmness or softness of baby Amanda's soft spot if pressure were building up. Ted and I were quite saddened when her soft spot closed up around eight months of age and we could no longer use it for head checks. We oftentimes joked with the nurses and doctors, asking if they would surgically keep that soft spot open for us! With her soft spot gone, we had to rely on her level of consciousness and other symptoms that we learned through the years to determine if her shunt were draining like it should. Vomiting was always a ready symptom, and as she grew older, she could tell us if she had a headache, which was another common symptom. But then there was this one time ...

Amanda was somewhere around nine months old. It was late evening, and we were feeding her the last bottle of the night before laying her down and going to bed ourselves. I was half asleep, dressed only in my bathrobe, resting on one end of the couch. Ted was on the other end with Amanda in his arms, feeding her a bottle of formula. When the bottle was empty and it was time to burp Amanda, something went wrong. Amanda went all stiff, with arms outstretched and her body rigid. Ted called to me, knowing something was wrong, but we could not figure out what.

As our panic increased, we were in that situation of frightening fear, of total lack of control and utter hopelessness, of being totally clueless as to what to do next. I remember passing Amanda back and forth between us like a hot potato, each hoping the other would have the magic touch to make her "normal." Like a

---
WHISPERS FROM GOD

Psalm 23:4 Yea, though I walk through the valley of the shadow of death, I will fear no evil for thou art with me.

tightening noose, we knew things were getting worse because we weren't even sure Amanda was still breathing. She was a stiff, rigid, unresponsive baby, just like a plastic doll. Although the emergency 911 system was in place in some areas of the United States at this time, it was not universally available across the states and not available in our city. Ted and I were in the kitchen, trying to decide who to call or what to do.

Did we know the phone number of the fire or police department? No, we did not. Ted grabbed the phone off the hook, and in his panic pushed "0" for operator. When the kind operator answered, Ted stammered into the phone, "My baby's stopped breathing." Out of sheer desperation, he was simply yelling "help" into the phone, and that poor operator probably had no clue as to who we were or where we were. Ted told me later that he had a vision at that moment of a small white casket. That's when he turned to me and cried, "We're losing our baby!"

Realizing the futility of the phone call with the operator, he put Amanda in my arms and said, "We're going to the emergency room." Now, Children's Hospital was a good twenty-minute drive into Detroit. We weren't going there. We knew it would take too long. There was a small little hospital in Trenton, just five minutes down the road. We both flew out of the door, into the car, and Ted started down the street like a madman. Our neighborhood had many twisting and diagonal streets. It was not your simple checkerboard of street arrangement. There was one street that divided into a "Y," with one arm dead-ending up against a grassy embankment that ran along the main road we wanted to get on, and the other arm converging down aways to, finally, merge onto the desired street. In the dark of night, in our panic and the quietness of our neighborhood at eleven o'clock, we went roaring down the street and took the wrong way at the "Y."

We were driving too fast to care or to stop or to turn around. We simply blazed our own trail and went flying up and over the curb, through the grass, and finally onto the main road to take us to the hospital. All along the way, I was holding Amanda while Ted drove, and he kept saying, "Is she still breathing? Is she still breathing?" And then we remembered the railroad tracks! What would be the chances of there being a train at this time of night on our flight to the hospital? Ted was already talking aloud about the route he was going to take if we encountered a train, but fortunately the tracks were quiet and the train issue didn't come up. All the while during this short drive, it felt like electricity crackled and snapped through the car as we drove in a fog of fear and images of little white caskets. In his panic and frustration during the drive, Ted kept reaching over with his right hand and whacking Amanda on her back, trying to "snap her out of it" or dislodge whatever had gotten stuck and made her stiff like she was. One time, he hit her pretty hard, and I remember yelling at him. We both felt so scared and frustrated and helpless.

Screeching into the drive of the hospital emergency room, Ted was out of the car first, and went running into the ER screaming, "My baby's stopped breathing, my baby's stopped breathing." Well, I wasn't out of the car with Amanda yet and they didn't see me right away, so their response was, "Well, go back to the car and get her!" It's funny in hindsight. Even funnier was the fact that I had left the house exactly as I had been on the couch—dressed only in my bathrobe. And I mean only. I was barefoot as well! I came running in behind Ted with Amanda in my arms. Sometime during that hurried ride down the road, she had "snapped out of it" and was breathing just fine. The nurses gave her a little oxygen, listened to her lungs, and observed her for a little while. They could find nothing wrong with her. Their explanation was that she probably had choked on her formula.

Ted and I were numb with exhaustion from our frantic trip to the hospital. Both of us had been scared out of our wits. We felt like we had just run a marathon while our lives and our daughter's life had passed before our very eyes—and now we were told simply that our baby had choked? *You have got to be kidding me*, I thought. I've never seen a baby choke like that before. With polite smiles and patronizing little pats of assurance, the emergency room gave Amanda the A-OK and discharged us home. Okay—so maybe she just choked and we're just dumb parents.

It wasn't more than a day or two later when it happened again. This time, it didn't last as long, and Amanda "snapped out of it" pretty quickly. We were pretty shook up, but in a way relieved. Ted and I were both sure that Amanda hadn't "choked" the other day. We knew it had to be something else. This time, instead of the local hospital, we took the long drive down to the Children's Hospital emergency room. Amanda had already recovered from this incident, but it was frightening enough and we knew it wasn't anything good or normal.

At the Children's Hospital emergency room, we waited forever to be seen. It would have been nice to have had "frequent visitor status" what with all our trips to the hospital, but Children's Hospital was a big-city hospital, with ever-changing nursing staff and hundreds of patients being treated in the emergency room each week. Because of its great size, as well as it being a teaching hospital, we had to retell our story at every hospital visit to the newest nurse or doctor in training. Amanda was not in immediate distress, and there were other, sicker kids, who needed to be seen first. When it was finally our turn, we explained to the nurse what had happened with Amanda, how she seemed to stop breathing and her body became rigid and stiff. I guess we were convincing enough because they decided to admit her for observation. I could still detect little smirky smiles as they looked at Ted and me. I felt like they were thinking we were probably some crazy, neurotic parents who were just freaking out at every little thing that occurred with our daughter. After getting through all the paperwork and passing on all kinds of information to the nurse in care of Amanda, Ted and I went home to get some much-needed sleep, with plans to return first thing the next morning.

We were up early the next morning and went straight to the hospital as planned. Of course, we knew what room we had left Amanda in the night before and went straight to it. As we walked into the room, it was as though a cannonball had hit us in the stomach as we gazed at the empty space where she and her crib had been the night before. It's like this big force suddenly squeezes your middle, and all the air is sucked out of your lungs. It hurts and you panic. Quickly finding a nurse, we asked where Amanda was. After a few confusing minutes, she checked with the other nurses and replied, "Oh, they transferred her to ICU. George was her nurse last night, and she gave him quite a scare. He was feeding her, and she stopped breathing and went all rigid." After checking the charts, it was noted that "the patient did just as the parents had described." Hallelujah! Score one for the parents! They thought we were nuts until Amanda did the same thing for them! I believe, from the reports I heard, that she totally freaked them out, and they even called a "code blue" and brought in the crash cart and everything. As the saying goes, "Seeing is believing," and that's just what it took for everyone to believe what Ted and I saw happen with Amanda.

These episodes were finally diagnosed as a kind of seizure, resulting from intracranial pressure. Yes, that's correct, another shunt surgery. They took her to surgery, put in a fresh new shunt, and Amanda never had another seizure. It was at this point I recall asking one of the nurses in the special clinic Amanda went to for spina bifida patients, "So, what else can go wrong? What else can happen?" She replied that we would be overwhelmed if we were to see a list of the possibilities. It was better not to be told all that might go wrong and to just wait and hope that most don't happen.

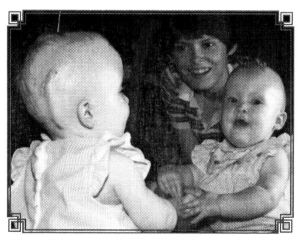

Amanda at about eleven months, with her shunt quite visible on her recently shaved head post-surgery.

There were many times throughout the years with Amanda that we, as parents, were made to feel ignorant. Every once in a while, we would just have to deal with doctors or nurses who were just so full of themselves and all of their book knowledge that they were sure they had all the right answers to our questions and that they always knew what was best for our daughter. As we would try to describe symptoms or various problems or occurrences to a medical person, it would become obvious that he or she wasn't really listening. And then there was that smug little smile that we would see as he or she tried to pat away our concerns with patronizing words.

THE HELPING HAND

Dear doctors and professionals: Please do not patronize parents, no matter how dumb or smart they appear. They are experts in the care of their child, and you must always listen to what they are trying to tell you.

To the doctors and nurses over the years who took our worries and questions seriously, who really listened and respected what we had to say about our handicapped child, whom we loved and cared for and wanted only the best for, Ted and I say, "Thank you."

8
TOTE-ing an Early Education

From the day of her birth, our worrying and wondering began about how much Amanda was going to be able to learn, accomplish, comprehend, and achieve. Because she was our first and only child at the time, she was always next to us, and we never stopped talking to her and interacting with her. Perhaps that is why, to this day, Amanda is such a social creature. Perhaps it is simply the personality that she was born with. Either way, I sometimes think she may have done better if she had been around the stimulation of other children her age. I have often thought that if Amanda had been our second or third child, maybe she would have picked up more "normal" behavior from older siblings. Instead, Ted and I were her entertainment. We sang songs and gave running commentaries on everything that was going on with Amanda and around her. Amanda listened and reacted to everything.

There was one quirky thing Amanda did that we never quite understood. It started somewhere around nine months of age. When Amanda was finished drinking her bottle,

Ted would say, "dead soldier!" If you are not aware, those words refer to an empty beer or wine bottle, and Ted would say it in the same context as "all gone!" The quirky part was that Amanda would start to frown when we said those words, after which she would howl and cry hysterically. At first, it was funny. After awhile, it got to the point where we had to make sure we didn't say it and to warn anyone who might be taking care of Amanda not to say it. This peculiar response didn't stop until bottles were stopped and we started introducing Amanda to drinking from sippy cups.

Instead of exploring her world through blocks, balls, and the quest to crawl, our Amanda explored her world by listening and reacting to all the songs, phrases, and verbal interactions that she could. If we tried to leave her by herself, sitting on the floor or in her highchair surrounded with toys in hopes of her actually playing with those things, she generally showed little to no interest in any of them. If toys were touched, it was to push them away. Next, Amanda would start whimpering and whining with practiced precision so as to catch our attention. Of course, we'd start talking to her and asking her what was the matter. If she wanted us to read a favorite book, she would hold it out to us and shake her little head enthusiastically up and down to command us to read it to her. Although she did not speak in words except for a *ya* and a *no*, she was a master at sad sighs, gleeful screams, happy giggles, and definite negative headshakes.

The first education program that Amanda took part in, when she was only a couple of months old, was called TOTE. It stood for Teach Our Tots Early. The TOTE program handled infant and toddler-aged children with multiple handicaps. I recall several women who worked for the program coming to the house once a week to work with Amanda. These women were physical and occupational therapists who specialized in early childhood development. They encouraged Amanda to do things that normal babies normally do without being taught—things like holding up their heads, rolling over, grasping objects, and stacking blocks.

Once a week, I could also go to a school and meet with other moms while the children played in another room. All of us moms had children with various handicaps and disabilities. We would sit in a circle and share the trials and successes of our children. You could tell that we all loved our children very much, and ached for someone to wave a magic wand and make our kids normal. It was nice to share in the company of other moms who struggled daily with the challenges of their special children. We all wanted our broken kids fixed.

THE HELPING HAND

Like any support group, there is great comfort to be found for parents of handicapped children to meet and share. They don't feel so alone.

The one and only main theme of those first TOTE years that I can remember was the advice to Ted and me to "stimulate Amanda." It was suggested that Ted and I should read to Amanda, talk to her, let her go places with us, and see and do everything we could think of. Well, we did that, of course. Again, I can't help but think that this left Amanda dependent on us for her entertainment. Perhaps we should have been a little bit more persistent at encouraging Amanda to find amusement in toys, rather than us caving so quickly to her unhappy whines. But since the toys weren't stimulating her, it was up to us to do just that. The TOTE program helped us watch and measure what Amanda could and could not do. This proved very beneficial, as it paved the pathway for Amanda to receive other services and gave us direction as to what education program was next available for her as she grew.

9

Give Baby a Year and See What She Can Do

On August 3, 1984, Amanda turned one year old. It had been a challenging first year, with close to a dozen surgeries on her shunt as well as life revolving around doctors' appointments and therapy sessions. Amanda was an adorable one-year-old and looked quite normal to any passerby. However, a passerby would probably guess her age to be around eight or nine months because Amanda was much smaller than average for her age. A normal one-year-old would be crawling, standing, and even walking. One would see this alert and happy little baby in her stroller—with fair skin and fine baby-blonde hair—and never know there was anything different about her.

As it was August and the weather was summery and hot, we had a backyard party for Amanda's birthday and invited all our friends. We had the party more as a celebration of thanks to everyone who had supported us throughout the previous year. Our dear friends had been so good to us by praying, cooking meals for us when Amanda was in the hospital, and just loving us and caring. It was also, of course, a celebration of Amanda making it through her first year.

Physically, Amanda wasn't doing a whole lot at this time. The best thing she could do was to sit! So whether she was sitting up in her high chair, on the couch, in the stroller, or on the bouncy horse she got for her first birthday, she sat tall and strong and looked like any other baby. Compared to life with a normal one-year-old, we had it pretty easy because we didn't have to chase a crawling baby on the verge of walking who was into everything. Wherever we went, we'd tote Amanda along and simply set her somewhere and she'd stay!

Amanda on her bouncy horse on her first birthday.

Amanda could sit and get herself engaged with whatever social interaction was going on. A sad little whimper, a small cry, or a squeal of laughter would cause anyone nearby to turn toward the little blonde baby making the sound. Amanda next would make eye contact and skillfully reel in her catch.

Amanda now had a live, talking toy to interact with. Toys made of wood or plastic were of no interest and, quite frankly, too much of a bother. They first had to be within reach because Amanda could not get to them. Then, they might be too heavy or too complicated for her inadequate thumbs to deal with. Due to another birth defect, which left her with poorly functioning thumbs, she had limited hand dexterity. It was too hard for her to play with toys.

She had five fingers on each hand, but the thumbs lacked the proper bone structure and length, leaving her with tiny ineffective mini-thumbs. Why did this happen? The best explanation I ever got from a doctor was that when you have a baby forming inside its mom and you get one birth defect, like Amanda's open vertebrae associated with her spina bifida, it throws off the natural course of development. Like dominoes set up in a great display of falling-down patterns, if one of the tiles falls wrong, it can mess up the whole proper sequencing. If one domino falls the wrong way, parts of the display are missed, and the desired progression of the whole project is botched. During the course of her development, Amanda's thumbs got botched. She could grasp with her other four fingers and did quite well managing a spoon and getting food into her mouth. But fine motor skills were pretty tricky and sometimes unachievable. You need a thumb to pick up Cheerios one at a time for eating. The pincer grasp is also quite helpful for putting puzzles together and getting buttons through buttonholes. Occupational therapists worked with her weekly, but we knew that hand surgery would have to happen someday.

Amanda's main form of entertainment at this age was social interaction. Because of the spina bifida, she could not crawl or walk. That meant she could not explore the room around her or get into any kind of mischief. Additionally, her lack of fine motor skills made playing with toys too challenging for her, and besides, she was just not interested. I suppose because she was always sitting by me as I worked around the house, shopped, or visited friends, I simply included her in what I was doing by always talking to her. I recall one time when Ted and I were shopping with Amanda in the stroller. As I shopped, I would constantly point things out to Amanda and talk to her. Ted had taken Amanda out of the stroller and was carrying her to go look at something else in a different part of the store when I caught myself pushing and talking to an empty stroller.

Since Amanda did not like to play with toys, when I took the time to sit and "play" with Amanda, it usually involved reading books to her. She loved being read to! From a pile of books, she would pull out the ones she preferred. Sitting quietly, she would follow along, while listening to every word that was read to her. She had her favorites, and they were read and reread countless times. You would think that with all the talking and reading I did, Amanda herself would be quite the chatterbox. But Amanda didn't talk in words. She could say "Mom" and "Dada," but her other baby gibberish was mostly incoherent to everyone but Ted and me. Of course, always in the back of our minds, we worried about Amanda's intelligence and whether she was going to think and learn like a normal person. She was already physically way behind the normal standards and not walking or performing gross and fine motor skills. She was small for her age and not growing much. Although she seemed to be listening, we worried about why she was not speaking normal, comprehensible words and whether she understood some or any of it at all.

It was a hot summer day once when I had just brought in the mail. Without air-conditioning, the house was steamy hot, and the heat was making me tired and cranky. Amanda was bored. I remember sitting down at the kitchen table and setting Amanda on my

---
THE HELPING HAND

Early childhood education and stimulation does pay off. However, it may take longer to see results with a special-needs child. Never give up.

---

lap. I started looking through the mail, and like I always did, talked to her about everything I saw. We were looking through the new Life magazine together, turning the pages and looking at all the colorful pictures when I stopped for a second on a big two-page ad for Marlboro cigarettes. There were men on horses galloping across the pages and "Marlboro" in big red letters across the top of the page. Amanda suddenly reached out with a finger and pointed at the "O" in Marlboro and said loud and clear and confident in her little tiny voice, "Oh!" Hallelujah and amen! I swear I heard the angels singing the "Hallelujah Chorus" right then. Amanda wasn't even two years old, and here she was recognizing letters. I was so excited and couldn't wait until Ted got home to tell him! It was like a fine mist of normalcy had suddenly entered the room on that hot summer day. I had visions of Amanda in school, reading and writing, just like any other kid. Maybe we *did* have a chance at her being normal like everyone else! It was a splash of hope.

We soon discovered that she actually knew all of the ABCs. For all the times we propped Amanda in front of the television show *Sesame Street* and for the gazillion times we read Dr. Seuss's ABC book to her, our efforts had finally paid off. We delighted in pointing at letters on buildings and street signs and asking, "What letter is that, Amanda?" and hearing her reply with the right answer! Her pronunciation wasn't always clear, but doggone it, she knew her letters! Ted and I were probably a little maniacal at this point with this silly name-the-letter game. But every time she answered correctly, it was as though we heard a "cha-ching" of coins as we tried desperately to fill the bank with normalcy.

Amanda loved being read to.

It soon became clear that, although Amanda knew and said letters as well as complete words, speaking so that others understood her words was clearly a struggle for her. Her speech was very choppy. She would leave parts of words out, such as one time when she wanted to try something on her own, the phrase "Amanda do it" came out as "Ah-dah do it." For a while we called her "Ahdah," because it was cute and a fun little nickname. But then we realized that she was accidentally leaving out the middle syllable of her name. Other words and phrases sounded like this as well. After a hearing test to make sure her lack of hearing wasn't the cause of her speech coming out so wrong, we started her with a speech therapist. Another therapist added to the list! Oh, she fit right in with the physical therapist and occupational therapist. But, amazingly, by the time she was three years old, Amanda's speech smoothed out and began to sound "normal." Cha-ching!

10
Should Amanda Have a Sister?

Life with one-year-old Amanda had fallen into a pleasant, normal routine. With her first year of multiple shunt surgeries behind us, we had become very comfortable with taking care of our daughter, and life seemed good. Amanda was, generally, a fairly happy baby, and for the most part, pretty easy to take care of. Because of her paralysis from about the waist down, Amanda didn't crawl, and of course, couldn't walk. She pretty much stayed where she was sitting. There were plenty of appointments to go to: she was getting both physical and occupational therapy, and we went quite frequently to the spina bifida clinic at Children's Hospital for checkups by her team of doctors, which included a urologist, neurosurgeon, orthopedic surgeon, and pediatrician, as well as a host of other professionals from social worker to nurse to the physical and occupational therapists. Again, it was our normal. Ted and I always knew we wanted more than one child, and we were ready to take on the responsibility of adding to our family. Several months after Amanda turned one year old, we started trying for our second child. This time,

I got pregnant right away. The due date for our second-born was to be within a week of Amanda's second birthday.

I'm sure there were many people who thought we were crazy to have more children. Specifically, I can recall one nurse whom I spoke with. Amanda was, again, in the hospital for some surgery, and I was obviously pregnant with another child. I can remember sitting next to Amanda's crib and taking care of her while a nurse, obviously pregnant as well, sat on the other side of the room, feeding a bottle to Amanda's hospital roommate. The nurse and I talked casually about different things, and then, I remember her getting an almost disdainful look on her face as she asked me how in the world I could even think about having another baby after having one like Amanda! I was stunned by her question. I don't even recall what I answered, but it definitely made me think.

> **WHISPERS FROM GOD**
>
> Jeremiah 29:11 *For I know the plans I have for you, declares the Lord, plans to prosper you and not to harm you; plans to give you hope and a future.*

Part of me was quite angered by her question. I thought, *Who does she think she is that she should question me?* Was she so sure that *her* baby was going to be perfect? How dare I bring another damaged baby like Amanda into the world? Wouldn't that have been a stunner for her to have a baby with challenges? But I also know that there are many parents who, after the birth of a handicapped baby, choose to have no more children. These parents throw themselves 100 percent into the care of their needy child. I guess that's a good thing. But I've also seen it as a bad thing, too. I've seen couples who are so engrossed in the care of their handicapped child that they lose interest in everything else, including their spouse.

Every thought, action, and life decision is made around the needs of the child.

I recall one time when Ted and I took our family to a party that was held at a racquet club. There were stairs to the upper level, where the party was, and no elevator. Like always, we did what we had to do, and the two of us carried Amanda and her wheelchair up the steps. There was another family there with a child in a wheelchair, and I remember them being outraged that there was no elevator. Yes, it would be nice for the handicapped population to have access to everything and everywhere, but sometimes you just have to make do; after all, our daughter truly was the minority. These parents were absolutely fuming angry with the demand that the world should change to accommodate their child. Personally, I don't find that to be a healthy attitude.

Of course, both Ted and I wanted the best for Amanda. We took care of her and her needs the best that we knew how, but sometimes being the best for someone means taking time for yourself as well. We felt sorry for these parents who were so angry that the rest of the world didn't share in the passion they had for their daughter. Ted and I will look for compassion and acceptance from others, but we don't expect everything to change so that the world revolves around Amanda. We were comfortable, at the time, with our daughter and her needs. We were certain we had room for more children in our family. Besides, I felt like I deserved a second chance for a healthy baby. Why should I be denied that privilege? And if my second baby were to be born with the same birth defects as my first, why then, I thought, I'd be so much better prepared and knowledgeable as to what to expect. Amanda would also have a sibling with a lot in common. Besides, what if I decided to not have more children, and one day when she was older, Amanda were to ask me why she didn't have any brothers or sisters? Was I really going to answer her, "Because I was afraid I'd have another one like you?" Ted and I wanted more children and were sure about increasing the size of our family.

With this second pregnancy, the doctor thought it would be best

> **THE HELPING HAND**
>
> *The decision as to how many children a couple should have is entirely personal and individual. Finances, available support system, and commitment are just some of the factors affecting the decision. Please don't judge what another family chooses.*

to have a little bit more notice about the health of our baby. Remember that we found out about Amanda's physical problems only two days before she was born. Early in my second pregnancy, the doctors performed an amniocentesis and drew off some of the amniotic fluid surrounding this baby. After testing the fluid, we would know whether or not this baby had spina bifida. Test results took a week or two. Of course, we prayed for a healthy baby. We also were hoping for that son we didn't get the first time. Finally, the phone call came. A healthy baby with no health problems! And it was a girl. Another girl. We were a little disappointed at first. For some reason, we were still stuck on that old-fashioned idea of the importance of having a son. An heir. But then I quickly came around to the thought that it would be great for Amanda

> **PASS IT ON**
>
> *According to the CDC, about one in every thirty-three babies is born with a birth defect.*

to have a sister, a same-sex sibling. They would have more in common and could play together. And personally, I never had a sister. I have just one older brother. I always thought how wonderful it would be to have a sister to share toys, thoughts, secrets, and life with. Perhaps because I never had that experience, God was blessing me with daughters so that I could watch and witness what I never had.

Two years and a day after the birth of our daughter Amanda, we welcomed our daughter Kristen Leigh Greshel into this world. Amanda's birthday was August 3, and now Kristen joined us on August 4! The circumstances around this birth were so different from Amanda's that it felt like it was happening for the first time. So much fear and anxiety surrounded the birth of Amanda. Plus, Amanda's birth was by C-section, and I never experienced labor. With Kristen, we already knew she was healthy, and the doctor was allowing me to attempt a VBAC—a vaginal birth after a C-section. Well, labor and pushing didn't end up being exactly a picnic, and the only difference between delivery by C-section and a typical delivery is when and where you want to hurt. Oh—and where the stitches need to go.

I went into the hospital at 6:00 a.m. and delivered Kristen at 6:00 p.m. And although they are sisters, Kristen and Amanda are quite different in appearance. Amanda is fair-skinned, with blonde hair and gray eyes; Kristen has brown hair and brown eyes. She also has more color in her skin than her fair-skinned older sister. So, everything from the circumstances of the delivery to the actual looks of each baby was completely contrasting. To me, however, the greatest contrast was the difference between their legs. Amanda had skinny little baby legs that did not move, although they twitched at times rather involuntarily and spasmodically. Kristen was born with legs that were long and strong. As someone once said about Kristen when she was a young girl and dancing on stage, "That Kristen has legs that go all the way to the floor!" Whereas most newborn babies prefer to be curled up, with legs and arms drawn up close to their bodies, newborn Kristen had her legs stretched out in front of her, as if she were glad to get out of that cramped space and finally stretch her legs! Kristen grew up to be the tallest of my three daughters, topping me by a few inches as well.

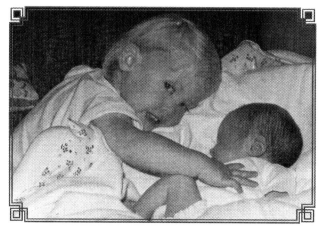

Amanda with newborn Kristen.

11
Hoping Your Broken Child Will Bloom

The Greshel family was now a family of four. Life was good. Amanda had been in good health, and there had been no hospitalizations for several months. Newborn Kristen was healthy and a good baby as well. It was the summer of 1985. Compared to other families with a two-year-old and a newborn, I probably had it easier than most. My two-year-old wasn't running around the house getting into everything. When baby Kristen needed to be fed, I sat Amanda on the couch next to me and read her books while Kristen nursed. Our family had settled into our own day-to-day routine; we were living a "normal" life.

Amanda was still very small for her age, so people who may have glanced our way in passing probably observed a mom and dad with two cute little daughters who appeared to be very close in age. Once Kristen was a few months old, I could prop her up in the double stroller with Amanda planted in the other seat, and off we'd go for walks around the neighborhood or shopping at the mall. At a glance, no one probably even considered that the little blonde girl couldn't walk. She was sitting so nicely in the stroller! At this young age, the differences in abilities between the two girls were there, but noticeable probably only to Ted and me. Especially since Amanda looked so much younger than she was, expectations from strangers were few, and the ability gap was not so obvious.

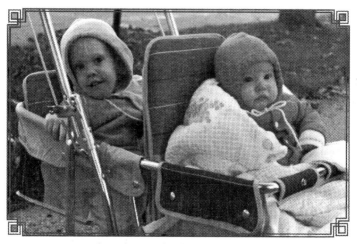

Amanda taking a backseat to sister Kristen.

Kristen was learning new baby skills all the time in the normal time frame of baby development. She was grasping toys at four months, rolling over easily at five months, and at eight months was jabbering "Momma" and "Dada." As Ted and I worked constantly to get Amanda to do more with her hands, say words with understandable clarity, and do more of the "normal" toddler things, our Kristen gained new skills constantly without any effort. It was like we were trying to nurture two flowering plants. The Kristen plant was happy and healthy and thrived in rain or shine. It grew and reached for the warm sunshine and put down strong roots. Growth was abundant, with new leaves sprouting and buds appearing everywhere on the stems. As Kristen grew, we just knew she was going to thrive and blossom someday into a beautiful mature plant.

The Amanda plant, on the other hand, started out challenged, with broken foliage. We had to constantly cheer it on while we hoped and prayed and pleaded for it to grow strong. It always seemed smaller and sickly, yet we were never sure of the right amount of water or fertilizer to give it. Every day we did our best and guessed at what we should do to it in hopes of seeing healthy growth and flourishing leaves. I can remember days, throughout the years, when I would look at the weak, struggling Amanda and just cry to God to let her blossom. With her future so unsteady and unknown, I would cry to God to help Ted and me enable Amanda to reach her greatest potential so she could bloom. I was always certain that we would someday discover her own great gift and ability, and I would plead to God to help us discover that. If I could just find the one thing that she was going to be good at, I would be willing to take her and that ability to the moon!

Everything seemed so easy for Kristen. Unlike Amanda, Kristen had normal fingers on her hands. Kristen effortlessly learned how to pick up bits of food, put puzzles together, grasp and play with toys, turn pages of a book, and execute countless other tasks requiring finger dexterity. Kristen also had the physical ability to crawl and walk, enabling her to explore her world and get to other places. For Amanda, her awkward thumbs, inability to use her legs for mobility, and questionable ability to learn made everything a challenge. It was hard for her to have to struggle in learning every new task, and hard for us to watch. But that was life in the Greshel house with baby Kristen and two-year-old Amanda.

Like most families of four, we were a ma and a pa with two young'uns to bring up. We were happy, for the most part, and doing the best we knew how.

Amanda and Kristen sometime in 1986.

12
Surgeries, Therapies, and How to Go: Learning to Stand

It was during the early toddler-age years that many corrective surgeries and therapies were taking place for Amanda. Therapists worked to teach her skills that she would need and was struggling to learn on her own. Despite her inadequate thumbs, Amanda had to learn to put food in her own mouth and to hold a fork, spoon, and cup. Putting on socks, gloves, or a jacket were skills Amanda needed to perform, along with zipping her jacket or buttoning her shirt. Therapists helped Amanda gain arm strength so that she could have the strength to scoot her seated body or even army crawl, using only her arms, short distances. Doctors were trying to surgically correct things early so that limbs would have a chance to grow normally. It was as if Amanda were my little rosebush, and she was being trimmed, pruned, and grafted so that she would grow correctly.

In particular, both of Amanda's hands and feet had their turn being "under the knife" while she was between three and five years old. At birth, Amanda's feet were both curled inward, probably because she couldn't stretch and move them. Her "clubfeet," as they were called, needed to be made straight and flat like regular feet if she were ever going to stand on them. Foot surgery was a breeze for all of us because Amanda had no feeling in her lower extremities. Post-op pain was not even an issue, so we didn't have to comfort a child in pain or even administer any pain medication. We were pretty much in and out of the hospital overnight for foot-straightening surgery. Following surgery, her feet were enclosed in plaster casts to maintain the surgically corrected position they were put in. Amanda could not walk anyway, so sitting with casts on her feet was not any different from sitting without casts on. The hardest thing to deal with in regard to this surgery was that Amanda was a bit heavier to pick up due to the added weight of the plaster, and trying to give her a bath was a challenge!

Amanda with both legs in casts.

Occupational and physical therapy was a weekly routine for Amanda. Occupational therapy helped Amanda perform tasks that dealt with the smaller, fine motor skills: building with blocks, putting puzzles together, as well as personal care tasks like brushing her teeth and combing her hair. These skills did not come naturally, as Amanda was learning to handle things with not-so-perfect thumbs. Physical therapy handled the larger, gross motor skills Amanda needed to actually move her body: learning to crawl using only her arms and learning to push up to a sitting position. Again, these were skills that did not come naturally because

PASS IT ON

Physical therapy focuses on balance, walking, and general movement. Occupational therapy helps patients with self-care needs and activities of daily living. The general and informal dividing line is: physical therapists work with the body from the waist down, and occupational therapists work with the body from the waist up.

spina bifida had taken away Amanda's ability to use her legs. Amanda was not a fan of either. Physical therapy was hard work, which required strength and practice. Amanda would get tuckered out and want to just lie on the exercise mat. Many goals were finally reached only after everyone else was exhausted from cheering Amanda on. Other times, success came after Amanda's temper tantrum and tears. Occupational therapy was sometimes easier for Amanda since it could be disguised as playtime. Manipulating puzzle pieces or buttoning buttons was not physically tiring, but if it got too difficult or boring, the tears of frustration would start flowing and Amanda would just quit.

Once a week I would make the drive down to Children's Hospital in Detroit for Amanda's physical and occupational therapy. Baby Kristen came along for the trip, too, since I had no daytime sitter who could watch her. Thankfully, Kristen was a low-maintenance baby, who traveled easily wherever we went. I would bundle up both nonwalking daughters and pack a bag with toys and snacks for both children to make the drive to the hospital. Depending on traffic and construction, It was a twenty to thirty-minute drive each way. I would park in the parking garage, load my babies into the double stroller, and then get us over to the therapy rooms in the hospital for Amanda's appointments. I would keep Kristen entertained while the therapists worked with Amanda. Afterward, I would bundle them all up for the long trip back home. It was a lot of work for this young mom with little ones! Eventually, we had therapists who came to the house. That made life quite a bit easier.

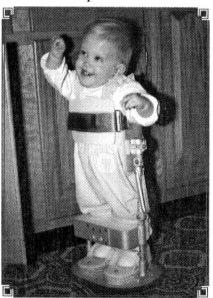

Amanda in her parapodium.

Physical therapy revolved around getting Amanda upright and moving on her own. Around this time, they crafted her a "parapodium." A parapodium is a contraption that allows a person to stand up. We would buckle and strap Amanda into it, and she could stand. There was a large oval base under her feet, bars and Velcro straps at her knees and hips, support at her backside, and support on her belly. The purpose was to give Amanda the same perspective as any other toddler who was on her feet, as well as to stimulate bone growth by forcing her legs to bear weight. We would stand Amanda in front of a table and place toys in front of her to play with. As usual, she showed no interest in any toys except for making a game out of removing everything in front of her. Once she threw everything off the table, we'd replace them for round two of the clear-the-table game. Amanda didn't really mind being in her parapodium, but we stayed close to replenish the toys she kept flinging and to make sure she didn't tip over.

Besides the gross and fine motor skills that were always being worked on and addressed, bowel and bladder issues for Amanda were changing and challenging. Incontinence is not so cute after age three or four. Emptying the bladder and moving the bowels become much trickier. The pushing on the bladder trick we used with infant Amanda didn't work anymore. It didn't always completely empty the bladder, and residual urine in the bladder contributed to a greater risk of bacteria growth.

THE HELPING HAND

Being in a wheelchair in public is now socially acceptable. It is not so much of a spectacle as it once was. Therapists and friends are quick to address and cheer on efforts to get a patient walking. For caregivers, incontinence has always been the bigger issue. It is not socially acceptable. It is also not talked about as much, and it is where we need the most help.

The result was a bladder infection. Over the years, Amanda

has had countless infections. It's just part of life with an incontinent person. So, we had to learn to catheterize her. I didn't want to learn how to do that. I knew that it was just going to add to my list of things that I had to do to take care of Amanda. It was also going to make it extremely challenging to find family or friends who would be willing to learn how to catheterize her so that Ted and I could ever get away. It also meant the need for a continuous monthly delivery of medical supplies from a medical supply store. Medical supplies get delivered to homes where sick and old people live. It's not normal.

The whole bowel process for Amanda continued to be just as challenging. As a baby, the chocolate laxative bottles were easy. Amanda liked the taste of them, and they were pretty reliable in causing the bowels to empty each morning. Unfortunately, they worked rather explosively, so that only a diaper could collect the results. It is not socially acceptable to be at school with a stinky, full diaper, and we were getting ready to send Amanda off to preschool. At first, the approach by the medical personnel at Children's Hospital was to train Amanda's bowels the "natural" way. One nurse thought if we put Amanda on the toilet every day at the same time and she pushed and pushed, that a bowel movement would happen. Of course, Amanda would have to eat all kinds of fiber-rich foods and drink lots of liquids to help with the process. High-fiber foods weren't exactly on young Amanda's favorite foods list. Show me a toddler who is not a picky eater and who will eat what you tell him or her to. This same nurse didn't want us to get in the habit of using laxatives, stimulants, or other "unnatural" ways to get her poop to come out. Through diet, timing, and Amanda learning to "sense" when she had to go, we were to achieve success. I really don't know what planet that nurse was from! Amanda was not normal, and she was not going to poop "au naturel."

At this time, our best options for getting Amanda's bowels to move were either suppositories or enemas. They worked the best because when you used them, you knew she was going to go shortly after. We couldn't depend on the timing of laxatives or fiber-filled foods for when we would get results. Pooping had to happen when we wanted it to. Getting Amanda to move her bowels daily and in a timely manner continued to be the great challenge. Despite our best efforts, there were still occasional accidents. If she ate more than usual and the last toileting had produced skimpy results, we'd get a surprise overflow blowout. There wasn't much we could do about it except clean up the mess and move on.

13
Looking for Help through Friends and in the Shower

Parenting is hard. It doesn't matter if your kids are normal and healthy or if they present with challenges. Decisions to make, circumstances that occur, choices taken, and all the bumps that happen on the road of life can make child-rearing a fun, crazy, frustrating, joyful, painful, and adventuresome road to travel. The road with Amanda has been one heck of a ride. I honestly don't know how I made it through some of those days, or even some of those weeks. There were many mornings when I would lose myself in a hot shower.

> ### WHISPERS FROM GOD
> Romans 3:23 ... *for all have sinned and fall short of the glory of God.*

Leaning against the tile wall with the hot water streaming down, I would imagine myself cradled in God's loving, safe arms and I would pour my heart out to Him. Some of those showers got pretty long because I just couldn't get out of the shower and face another day.

As a parent of a handicapped child, I can tell you that I needed help. I didn't always get it. Many times I yearned for someone who would listen to me when I needed to vent. Most of the time and even now, twenty-nine years into Amanda's life, I feel like a pot simmering on the stove because of all my pent-up feelings. The emotions and pain just keep simmering under the lid as I hold them inside. Many times I feel like I am going to explode.

The weekly meetings with the other TOTE moms helped some. There was comfort in being with other moms of challenged kids. Each meeting began with a formal, polite friendliness between moms. As our meeting time progressed, we often got more relaxed and informal, as the talk would turn to more personal issues with our children. Meetings would end with cheers and tears as we would celebrate accomplishments achieved by our children but often cry with sympathetic understanding of each other's challenges.

There was also a spina bifida group that met once a month at the Children's Hospital in Detroit. We attended when we could and made several friends of other families with spina bifida children. One problem with the families we met here was that they came from a rather large radius surrounding the metro Detroit area. As we were a half-hour south of Detroit and our new friend might be a half-hour north of Detroit, distance and infrequency of the group meeting made it hard to produce many lasting friendships. This spina bifida group eventually stopped

---

PASS IT ON

The Internet has made it simple to find local support groups. Information on support group activities is available at your fingertips, and new friends can be made with daily computer exchanges.

Laurel Rausch Greshel

meeting. I have noticed that these groups are available again today, twenty-some years after our relationship with them.

They are thriving because the Internet has allowed a group of people who are distanced by miles and meeting times to talk and interact on a daily basis through computer connections. Ted and I still had plenty of friendships established from our church and neighborhood relationships. Many of my

PASS IT ON

Besides locating local support groups, an Internet search can connect you with national and international online support groups through Yahoo, Facebook, and other organizations with their own websites.

friends were also young moms, with busy homes of one or more children. I am not aware that I was ever excluded from get-togethers of moms and kids; we were always with other families at the park, the pool, birthday parties, or the library. Like typical moms, we shared stories about what our picky kids were or were not eating, how long nap time lasted, if our child slept in his or her own bed the night before, or the adorable new thing our baby did the day before. I could pretty much join in these conversations because I had stories to share about Kristen even if I couldn't tell a normal one about Amanda.

Although I had the support of other moms around me, I did not have a mom of a special-needs child to share special problems with. I don't think I would have had much participation in a conversation about how we spent an hour in the bathroom that morning trying to get Amanda's bowels to move, or how I was not looking forward to a day full of hospital tests for Amanda the next day. I didn't want to bring up those things because I knew the other moms could not relate. And I didn't want to talk about those and other things simply to get their sympathy. Besides, I was sure the others wouldn't understand. I suppose I was trying to fit in with the other families and come across as normal.

In addition, as both a parent of a special-needs child and a Christian, there is a burden to live up to. People expect Christian parents of handicapped children to be almost mini-saints. There is a false impression that Christians have it all together—that we are saintly and serene because we have the peace of God within us. Oh, there are countless times that God has helped me through situations. He does help me find peace and strength. I know He has carried me through tough times when I felt that I couldn't go on another step. He has blessed me with so much through the care and love of family and friends. But although a Christian, I am also human. I have struggled, cried, cursed, and behaved quite badly at times. Thank goodness, when I am at my worst, God is at His best.

There are times when my human weaknesses show themselves, and I am cranky, tired, impatient, and just downright mean. I worry and wonder what people think of me when they see me like that. Do they question my faith? Do they take note of how this professed Christian is acting so unchristian-like? On the days when I am tired of being the caregiver, when my body is tired or aching, or my faith wavers, I hope people understand and do not condemn. God is indeed faithful, and I know I would not have made it all these years without trusting and believing in Him. Although my dirty human flaws have sometimes made a public display, I pray my faith in Christ cuts through the grime and shines through as a testimony to His greatness.

Through the years, help came, or didn't, in many different forms. As a young mother of newborn Kristen and two-year-old Amanda, I was lonely at times. Ted and I lived in Michigan, with no other family close by. There was a woman at our church whom I'll call Louise, or Lou for short. She took me under her wing, almost like a daughter, and showed me great compassion. She was like my surrogate mother. On warm days, I would load baby Kristen and two-year-old Amanda into the stroller and walk over to "Grandma Lou's" house. The visits got me out of the house, and I got to visit and talk to motherly Lou. Several times, Grandma Lou even let me drop the kids off at her house so I could manage a trip to the store or to the dentist by myself. She was my mom refuge.

I don't know if I did something wrong or if Grandma Lou got tired of my visits, but after several months, Lou became consistently unavailable. Phone calls went unanswered. Several times when I walked over, I would find the front door and windows open, but when I knocked on the screen door, Lou wouldn't answer. In my naïveté, I assumed she went for a walk or a quick trip to the store. It wasn't unusual to leave doors open and unlocked in our neighborhood. But the relationship literally had been cut off. It wasn't until months later that I realized that Grandma Lou was probably home and she simply didn't want to answer my phone calls or my knocking at the door. It hurt that my surrogate mom

> **THE HELPING HAND**
> *Caregivers need support, and it can come as easily as a friendly pair of listening ears.*

> **THE HELPING HAND**
> *If a parent or caregiver takes up too much of your time, you may gently set limits. We don't mean to overwhelm you.*

didn't want me to visit anymore. I welcomed and needed those visits. We haven't spoken since. I'm sorry I was such a pest.

This chapter began with the words "Parenting is hard," and I would like to restate and clarify that the statement pertains to any parent of any child, handicapped or not. In a parent's pursuit of being a good mother or father, I think we have to find the support we need, spend time with other parents, read whatever books we can find on the subject, and ask for help and advice from friends and family. Keep searching for people you can relate to. Forgive those who move away, either physically or emotionally. And remember to give support, advice, and love back to others whenever you can.

14
Give a Three-Year-Old a Wheelchair: Walking Braces

Amanda got her first wheelchair when she was three years old. It was amazing to see, as she sat in it for the first time, how she was able to immediately start pushing herself around. Ted and I were flabbergasted! Apparently all the work with her therapists had given her the strength she needed to move her chair. We didn't have to teach her; she just started wheeling where she wanted to go. She giggled and gleefully pushed her chair where she wanted it to go. It was as though little Miss Amanda had been harboring this secret ability of wheelchair mobility.

THE HELPING HAND

Doctors and professionals who work with special-needs children or physically disabled adults need to realize that parents and caregivers need every detail of explanation for new treatments of care. The world you work in every day is a foreign land to us, and you need to tell us about all the little things—even seat belts.

After first picking up Amanda's new wheelchair, Ted and I stopped at a local shopping mall, where we knew they had a pet shop. We also had one-year-old Kristen with us, and we knew the girls loved visiting the fish and puppies. Amanda was getting along great using her new wheelchair in the pet shop until she leaned forward to take a closer look at some fish. She had stopped in front of an aquarium and had called us to come look at the fish she was observing. As she leaned toward the aquarium, she fell forward and straight out of her chair onto the ground! The people at the wheelchair place let us leave with our three-year-old in her first wheelchair without a seat belt! We didn't know any better because this was all new to us! On the way down, Amanda's head smacked some sharp-edged molding, which made a very definite bold red line on her forehead. A little bit of a harder hit, and it would have split right open. Amanda cried and cried as Ted and I looked at each other and wondered how we got out of that wheelchair place without someone recognizing the need for a seat belt!

From the day she was born, I always hoped that Amanda would one day be able to walk. That seemed like my ultimate goal for her. If she could only walk, she would be normal and just like everyone else. It was such a thrill to see her standing in her parapodium, because otherwise, Amanda was always just sitting. She sat on the couch, she sat in a high chair, she sat in her wheelchair, and she sat wherever we plunked her little butt down. To see this little blonde-haired cutie standing upright just gave fuel to the vision of her walking and then running around the house. Amanda's legs always twitched and moved a little. It was always my thinking that one day all the nerve connections were going to fuse and repair themselves and Amanda would just take off on her own two feet.

For several years, the physical therapist actually tried to get Amanda walking. Leg braces were made for her. They fit on her legs from toe to hips and were connected at her back with bracing and cables.

PASS IT ON

The kind of leg braces that Amanda used, which are often successful for spinal cord injuries, are the RGO— or Reciprocating Gait Orthosis.

Using a walker, Amanda was taught to lean on her left foot, and then kick her right foot forward using a push from her torso and hips. The right foot would swing forward, and Amanda would then lean her weight onto that right foot, so she could next swing the left one forward. It was not Amanda's favorite thing to do. It was quite a lot of hard physical work. She did this "lean and swing/kick" motion while holding on to a walker. We actually have videotape of her walking along the sidewalk in front of our house with her braces and walker. But Amanda never liked walking in this manner. It was slow, hard work. And she couldn't sit and rest with the braces on. To lose her step or footing also meant she could fall down. Her hands were never free to do anything, because she was holding on for dear life to the walker.

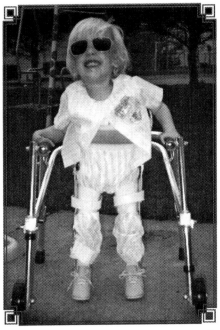

Amanda in her Reciprocating Gait Orthosis.

As excited as Ted and I were about Amanda's "walking," we soon realized it wasn't practical for her. In her wheelchair, Amanda could go almost anywhere. There was no fear of falling down, and she could wheel up to a table to get at any task at hand.

Like most young people who are wheelchair users, Amanda learned to pop wheelies in her wheelchair. She loved showing off this trick to any audience. The chair had wheelie bars, which enabled her to pop a wheelie and rest on the bars in a tipped-back position. Being the social little people-person that she is, Amanda learned to use this trick to get attention. The way she did it was a little bit wicked. Amanda would hang out at store entrances, where there would be a busy stream of shoppers coming in and out. For some reason, Amanda chose little old ladies for her performance. She would catch them walking in her direction and then suddenly snap her arms to flick herself into a fast backward tip. The innocent passerby would fear that this small child was falling backward to a painful landing and would lunge forward in an attempt to catch Amanda's chair. The poor victim of Amanda's trick usually grabbed her chest in a sigh of relief as Amanda giggled at her proud performance.

Being small meant that Amanda's wheelchair was also small. This was a lovely thing, because she and her chair fit easily through every doorway in our house. Even today, Amanda is still in a small chair, and we have never had to open up doorways

THE HELPING HAND

Sometimes you have to abandon your hopes for reaching an ordinary goal with a handicapped child and give in to what works best for him or her.

or widen hallways to accommodate her chair. Amanda was much more "handi-capable" in her wheelchair, and we finally resigned ourselves to the fact that our daughter wasn't going to walk. We learned later that other issues were going to make her more handicapped than not being able to get around on her own two feet.

15

The Family Grows Again:
Sending a Four-Year-Old Off on a Bus

It was 1986, and life was good for the Greshel family of four. Ted was the working daddy, and I was the stay-at-home mom. With August birthdays, Amanda turned three that year, and Kristen was a one-year-old. Kristen was a happy baby, who thrived and grew like any other healthy baby girl. She played with her sister, Amanda, and happily followed along to doctors' appointments and tolerated therapy sessions.

Amanda now had a sibling to play with. The challenge of taking the two of them places was not too great. The double stroller made it possible for me to go anywhere with them. As I already stated, Amanda was three years old when she got her first wheelchair. Kristen was walking by this point, so I had options of still using the stroller or letting Kristen walk while Amanda got around in the wheelchair. She could maneuver the chair herself for short distances without tiring. Amanda's shunt was behaving, and the foot surgery was behind us. Although thankful for things running so smoothly, Ted and I always found ourselves scared when things were going so well. Having already experienced how life could change overnight, we were careful to not overly celebrate the good times for fear that it would perhaps jinx things. We were respectful of the good times, but cautious not to celebrate too greedily.

Ted and I were ready to add to our family. Having grown up with just one sibling, I always knew that I wanted at least three children because two just wasn't enough. Ted had two siblings, so I believe he thought that three children was just right. Besides, maybe we'd finally get that son we wanted. With the challenges we had and those we knew we were going to face with raising Amanda, I believe we both knew that this was our last chance at having a boy. We never discussed baby number "four" because we both knew that three was going to be enough for us.

Soon after deciding that we were going to add to our family, I became pregnant with baby number three. It was a normal pregnancy like my previous one, quite unremarkable. Again, we had testing done and soon found out we were expecting another healthy baby—another healthy baby *girl.* Dashed, again, were the dreams of having a son. But at this point, it really didn't matter to Ted and me anymore. After having two girls, well, we felt like we were getting pretty good at raising girls! I'm not sure we'd know what to do with a boy, anyway. Fortunately, Ted wasn't much of a sports fan, so the lack of a basketball-dribbling, football-passing, and television game-watching buddy was not a loss that was felt. Girls were just as much fun, and they could play sports, too, if they wanted. I rationalized that now I could pass on clothes and toys to a third daughter. But what really made my heart glad was that now we would have two "normal" healthy girls who could grow up together and share life experiences, as well as have the experience of a handicapped sister.

I am sure there were many people on the outside looking in at us who thought we were taking on more than we could handle. As during my pregnancy with Kristen, there were some who worried that spina bifida might happen again. Others probably thought of me as selfish for having another child when I was already consumed with the care of my special-needs firstborn as well as a second baby. For Amanda's two other sisters who may be reading this, I know the road hasn't always seemed fair or easy for you to have grown up with a special-needs sister, but be thankful that we had room in our hearts and home for more children. We planned for you and wanted you. In another situation, you might not have had the chance to be formed or born.

Two months after Amanda turned four years old and Kristen turned two, Jillian Tate Greshel joined our family on October 10, 1987. Labor and delivery went more easily and swiftly than with Kristen. And, once again, I had a baby girl so different from her sisters. Jillian was fair-skinned with brown eyes. Her hair, at birth, was a light brown with red in it. At birth, Jillian almost seemed angry, and came into this world with a little bit of an attitude. She would prove to be a very active and curious little girl, always looking for the next excitement. Jillian was the enthusiastic little bundle of energy that helped to assure us that three children was going to be just enough for our family.

Four-year-old Amanda with two-month-old Jillian.

Amanda started in the public school system in the same fall that Jillian was born. Amanda was four years old at the time. Where we lived, certain cities took on various handicaps. The hearing-impaired were seen at one school, the mentally challenged went to another school in another city, and POHI kids went to school in the city of Taylor. That's what Amanda was classified as: Physically and Otherwise Health-Impaired, or POHI for short. The "physically impaired" part of Amanda was her obvious wheelchair use, but included her surgically altered hands. Steps at the school or rough terrain on a school outing kept Amanda segregated from the other students. Gym class, jump rope, and playground slides and swings were not activities she could be part of. Amanda's hands did not easily learn the skills of using scissors, writing her letters, or completing art projects. The POHI program offered the assistance of therapists and paraprofessionals who would help find adaptive ways for the student to learn these skills. We were also watching Amanda's cognitive abilities and measuring her ability to learn. That was the "otherwise health-impairment" part of POHI. Amanda knew her ABCs and was able to read a little, but simple math skills were confusing to her. She also struggled with retelling a story after being read to. There were definite issues evolving for her capacity to learn. Because of both the physical deficits and the potential learning disabilities, the POHI program was where Amanda needed to be. It would identify problems and help with solutions, either through therapists or tutoring.

The city of Taylor, where the POHI students went, was ten miles from where we lived. A little yellow school bus, with a lift on it for her wheelchair, would come every day to bus her to school. I have to be honest: on the one hand, it was quite nice to have her going to school every day because it gave me a break from taking care of her. On the other hand, it was a bit uncomfortable sending a four-year-old off to school on a bus. The program started out with kids at preschool age, so off Amanda went to school

Life was busy for the Greshel family now that we had three little girls. I truly believe it is God's plan that people marry and have families while we are still young, because when the late thirties and forties came, I don't believe I would have had the energy for those busy years! Jillian had all the needs of a newborn, which included waking for nighttime feedings and diaper changes. Her needs alone left this mom sleep-deprived! Kristen was an active two-year-old, who was of the potty-training age as well as being very busy with plenty of youthful energy and curiosity. And then there was Amanda, who needed help with dressing, toileting, and just about everything. There were also the therapists who came to the house and doctors' appointments at Children's Hospital in Detroit. Life revolved around the needs of three daughters. No, I don't think it revolved; it was more like it spun!

The Greshel family, December 1987.

16
Hand Surgeries and Massive Casts

With foot surgeries behind us and a shunt that was behaving and not requiring any surgical fixes, it was time for the hand surgeon to take his turn. The hand surgeries were not so simple to get through. For whatever reason, Amanda was born with incomplete thumbs. She had five fingers on each hand, but the thumbs were tiny and in the wrong position on

_____

PASS IT ON
_____

The surgery to create a thumb from an index finger is called "pollicization."

her hands. Her thumbs stuck out higher on her hands, nearer to the index finger; and although they had bones in them, they were not attached to any hand bones. The big problem was she had no pincer grasp—you know, the thing that separates us from the chimps. She could not use her thumb and first finger to pinch and pick up a coin, raisin, or any small item. The surgical plan was to lop off the unusable thumb, and rotate, shorten, and reattach her index finger into a position to turn it into a thumb. The end result would be three fingers and a thumb. There would be no more counting to ten on her fingers.

Each hand was done in separate years so as to give time for each to heal and to allow the occupational therapists time to help Amanda learn to use her new thumbs. Both of these surgeries were long because of the time and intricacies of shortening tiny finger bones, moving and reattaching tendons, reshaping skin to cover the changes, and holding everything together with sutures and pins. Like her foot surgeries, Amanda would come out of surgery with a plaster cast on her arm to keep everything protected and in place while things healed. The hospital stay was usually just overnight. Pain medication, miraculously, was needed for maybe only a couple of days.

Imagine the challenges of a plaster cast on the arm of a three-year-old, and again on a five-year-old. Remember, this was not a normal little girl! Here was little Amanda, already slowed down by not being able to walk, and now we took away one of her hands! Also keep in mind that you might think that a person with her arm in a cast would have fingers sticking out on the end. That would be the case if the cast were holding together broken arm bones. Amanda, though, had broken, reattached finger bones, so her cast completely encased her hand. It looked like a huge white plaster club.

Amanda with her club cast.

It takes two arms with hands for a person in a wheelchair to push his or her chair. Unless she wanted to simply wheel in circles, Amanda could not get any distance on her own in her chair with one arm in a cast. With her younger sister running around her, Amanda did her best to keep up, but had to wait for a helpful push if she got too far away. This wasn't much of a problem if we were at home, but at the mall or school, someone had to help push her. Amanda has never been one to hurry or ever wheel fast enough to make a breeze in her hair, so for the most part, her lack of mobility didn't upset her too much unless she thought she was missing something fun. Besides, every kid at school and sympathetic passerby was always willing to give her a push. All she had to do was start turning and twisting around looking for somebody and then call him or her to help.

Smaller tasks that required just hands were another issue. If she wanted to eat or turn

---

THE HELPING HAND

Please try not to stare at the handicapped. They know you are staring. It makes them squirm, it makes them itchy, and it makes them sad.

95

the page of a book, Amanda again had only one hand to complete the task. Handling a spoon with one hand was doable. But drinking cups could not be too large or heavy to lift single-handedly. If Amanda did end up struggling with a certain large task, she would whine after a few seconds and perhaps make a feeble plea for help, then simply give up on the task at hand.

It was amusing to watch how, at first, Amanda would struggle to lift and move her arm because of all the extra weight of the cast. As time went on, her shoulder got very strong and she was able to really swing her plaster-encased arm. Both her sisters are lucky Amanda didn't wallop them at one time or another! But, by far, I think the most amusing thing that ever happened with Amanda while we were getting through hand surgery and recovery was this: Oftentimes there were things about Amanda that would make a stranger stare at her. Whenever there were shunt surgeries, she often had stitches on her head that were quite visible, either because they were near the front of her head or she didn't have enough hair to cover the incision area. We had plenty of stares over head stitches, where I'm sure people were horrified by imagining that the bad parents of this little girl had probably been neglectful and dropped her on her head! After several trips out shopping with Amanda riding in the stroller and her huge plaster club arm propped in front of her, Ted and I really were getting tired of the stares. After glancing at Amanda first with shock, then pity, people would cast their judgmental eyes to us with disgust as they imagined the horrible abuse we must have submitted our child to. We fixed them. Ted was pushing Amanda in the stroller one day while we were walking through the local shopping mall. After suffering several stares from passersby, he waited for the next one and promptly blurted out for the stranger to hear, "Amanda, you better be good, or I'm going to break your other arm!" We gave them what they were thinking and had a good laugh about it.

Through the years, Amanda continued to see an occupational therapist so that she could work on her hand skills. Amanda was not a fan of occupational therapy. At first,

WHISPERS FROM GOD

Luke 6:37 *Do not judge, and you will not be judged. Do not condemn, and you will not be condemned.*

it was fun for Amanda because so much of it was disguised as "play." Amanda would sort shapes, put puzzles together, and handle other small, fun items. She had therapy as a baby before any hand surgeries to help her cope without an opposing thumb, therapy after surgery while one hand was in a cast to help her deal with having only one hand available, and therapy after the casts came off to help her use her newly constructed thumb. The fine motor exercises continued to get more difficult as we tried to get Amanda to pull a button through a buttonhole, zip zippers, cut out things with scissors, hold a pencil and write, use a knife and fork with her food, plus many other fine motor tasks.

I can recall many therapy sessions sprinkled with tears as Amanda gave in to frustration as she attempted each difficult task. To Amanda, if it was too hard to do, it just wasn't worth doing. She didn't care. If she couldn't do it, she wouldn't continue to try to do it. Challenges would quickly frustrate her, and she'd switch to doing something that required less effort. To this day, Amanda is easily frustrated with tasks that come as new challenges. A new wheelchair seat belt or a new jacket with an untried zipper will cause Amanda intense stress. She will give it a try, sweat profusely, moan and groan, get teary-eyed, and then finally yell at the challenge set before her and roll away in her wheelchair in utter frustration, resigning from the impossible task. The whole trial episode may have lasted thirty seconds.

Over the years, I have become more frustrated at the things Amanda can't do than she has. I could never understand why she gave up so easily. Didn't she want to tie her shoes, put the LEGO's together, peel the potato, knit the scarf, string the beads, or handle the hamster by herself? Of particular frustration to me was why she couldn't or wouldn't learn to handle a catheter by herself so she could cath herself, instead of relying on someone else. We would tell her, if she only could learn to cath herself, then she could spend the night at a friend's house and be more independent!

As I think back, I realize Amanda has really never said to me, "I wish I could do this," or "I wish I could do that." It was always me pushing her and asking, "Why can't you do this?" or "Why can't you do that?" Perhaps my frustration comes from Amanda not pursuing the same goals I think she should. It's like she has always been accepting of herself and her own inabilities.

I have come to surmise that life in general is just one huge challenge for Amanda. Everything takes extra effort. Why would she want to take on anything else new and challenging? I think a big difference in outlook is that

THE HELPING HAND

Therapists make goals for patients to strive for. Don't be surprised if the patient sets his or her own goals.

if a normal, healthy person were to suffer an injury that would leave him or her wheelchair-bound and dependent on help from others, he or she would greatly desire to regain independence and would work like crazy to get back to doing what he or she could do before the injury. But Amanda was born the way she is. Everything she can do for herself came with great effort and learning. And if it was too hard to do, then she must have figured that it wasn't worth doing.

17
Why, God?

One constant question that always hovered in my mind in response to circumstances with Amanda was, "Why me?" It actually started in the first days after Amanda's birth, with my in-laws' glee in telling us how lucky we were. With all we'd been through with Amanda, and now adding more responsibility with a second and third child, we obviously asked God that question quite often. "Why me?" "Why us?" "Why did you give us a handicapped child?"

Sometimes on days when I was weary and depressed from taking care of all Amanda's needs, as well as tending to young Kristen, even younger Jillian, and the household chores that needed to be done, I would lift my tearful eyes to God and ask, "Was I bad?" This was a recurring thought of mine. Had my past of wicked deeds and unfaithfulness to God made Him so mad at me that now I needed to be punished? Amanda had not lived long enough yet to have racked up any sort of sinful past. She was certainly the innocent here. That only left me. And though I was sure I'd done my share of awful things, I could not understand why I got such a big penance.

This feeling of being bad continues to come up even to this day. When it's been a challenging day or week and I feel more tired or beaten up than usual, I look to God and ask why He is making it so hard for me. Being mother to Amanda is both physically and emotionally exhausting as I strive daily to make her happy, keep her healthy, and help her grow to her fullest potential. At the same time, I had two other daughters who needed a mom who could give them a healthy, loving upbringing, too. I understand that life can't be that easy for Amanda. It is because of her handicaps, because of a mother's love for her child, maybe even because I sometimes pity her, that I know I have to continue taking care of her. But as I strove each day to help, mold, and encourage her, another surgery or bad school report would beat me down. A person can only be thrown so many times against the wall before he or she crumbles.

Amanda must really get tired of her constant life of challenges. And I get weary from the constant attention I give to her needs. I want to shout, "Hey, God, we could use some help down here." I would really enjoy a break from my constant service to Amanda's requirements. And Amanda really deserves a few effortless things in her life, whatever they may be.

Another "why" question I ask myself from time to time is: Why did God choose Ted and me for this task of raising Amanda? If you, dear reader, are also the parent of a child with challenges, do you also get the comments such as, "Oh, you guys are so good!" "You two are such saints!" "God sure knew what he was doing choosing you two." "You guys are so special!" I've heard all those comments over the years. Quite frankly, while I try to respond kindly to the person making these comments, inside I want to scream! What if I were to respond to people by saying, "Yes, I am so good! What a saint I am! Ted and I wanted this and asked for it! Bring it on! We are God's chosen, and our sainthood has gotten us guaranteed seats close to God in heaven! Yeah, man!" Let's face it, no one gets pregnant and prays for a broken child! Would you volunteer for that? I don't think so! I certainly didn't volunteer. And for all those who have called me a saint or someone special? Well, that just makes me laugh my butt off! Personally, I think that when people come up to Ted or me and tell us about how wonderful we are for being Amanda's parents, I think they are actually thinking in their heads about how glad they are that it was us and not them! Perhaps the comments are made out of pity. Perhaps they are genuine and said out of pure kindness. Either way, I think people need to realize that, like other parents, we did not choose this.

So let's get back to that "Why me?" question. The only answer that I've found that I can live with is another question: "Why not me?" This is not a perfect world we live in. It is a sinful world, which started way back in the Garden of Eden. Man makes bad choices. Bad things happen. I recall hearing someone preach once that if being a Christian and following Christ meant that we would never have bad things happen to us, then we'd all choose to be Christians for the wrong reason. Everyone would choose to be a "Christian" and follow Christ so that he or she could have that umbrella of protection. It would be like joining a club or a gang so you could enjoy special members-only privileges. That's not God's plan. By grace alone, we are saved. And sin in this world allows all kinds of things to happen to all kinds of people. Which brings us back to the question of it not being "Why me?" but rather "Why not me?" Some days, I hate that He chose me to be Amanda's mom. I don't know what I'm doing sometimes. I don't want to do the job. I'm tired of the burden. I don't understand His plan. Can you see how I'd want to scream when someone smiles at me and calls me a saint? On other days, I can find peace in knowing that it's all part of God's plan. I may not like it, but I can accept it. But then I always keep this mental list of all the questions I'm going to ask God when I get to those pearly gates. Why me? Why Amanda? Why, why, why? I can't wait to hear all the answers. All the confusing pieces of life will suddenly fit together, like a puzzle, and the resulting picture will be perfect and whole. I'll be able to finally say, "Ohhh! So *that's* why you did it!"

18
Schoolmates Come and Schoolmates Go

Life at this time was busy, fun, lively, and falling into a somewhat normal pattern for the Greshel family. With needy baby Jillian, busy toddler Kristen, and my funny little Amanda, this family was doing pretty well. I was grateful for the break I got with Amanda attending school each day. Early education gave Amanda the boost she needed in learning her numbers, her colors, and other basics. It also gave her plenty of opportunities to socialize with other students. There were several special friends in this special school program. Some I will never forget.

Amanda had a darling little classmate I'll call Lyle. Through the years, we have seen many of Amanda's friends give up their lives here on earth. Each one lived a life so very precious and special. I have changed their names for the sake of privacy, but I must share a little about each one of them. Amanda was only about six or seven years old. Lyle was the same age as Amanda, and had spina bifida like her as well. He wore handsome little boy glasses and had shiny dark brown hair. His mom and I spoke occasionally in passing at school. Our lives shared similar challenges as we tried to get the best for our children through the public school system, tried to keep our children healthy, and had the highest hopes for our children's futures. We also shared many of the same doctors, as we both got medical care for our children at Children's Hospital in Detroit. One day, I was at the hospital with Amanda for a checkup at the clinic that included some sort of X-ray or scan. As we got off the elevator, Lyle's mom was rounding the corner in a hurry as she followed the gurney carrying her son's small body.

I was so happy to see a familiar face and greeted her with a cheery smile and a "Hi! What are you doing here?" With fear and concern on her face, she spoke quickly as she continued to follow the gurney. "Oh, it's not good," she replied. I recall her saying something about his bowels and an obstruction, and then she was gone. A few days later, I learned that Lyle had passed away. I was in shock. I felt so sad. This little boy was absolutely darling. Now he was gone. I couldn't believe it. It scared me so. This lovely, young, fresh, adorable child, who happened to have spina bifida, had succumbed to his physical handicaps and related health problems. It could have been Amanda.

Around the same time, Amanda also had a friend in the POHI school program named Marleena. Marleena had spina bifida as well, but she seemed so much more able than Amanda. Leg braces from the knees down enabled Marleena to walk. She was able to go places and do things that wheelchair-bound Amanda could never do. Dimple-faced, with a mop of thick red hair, Marleena was an energetic little spitfire of a girl. Amanda went to play at Marleena's house several times, and we got to know her whole family a little bit. Twice, Amanda went to summer camp with Marleena.

I remember feeling jealous sometimes of how physically able Marleena was. Oh, how I wished Amanda could walk like she did! Over the years, we lost track of Marleena, as the girls lived in different cities. She, like Lyle, also received care at Children's Hospital in Detroit. Our paths would cross again during the high school years.

We were always making new friends. There were Amanda's schoolmates at her school in Taylor. There were the friends her sisters had in Trenton. We had our church family. Even Ted's work associates came to know Amanda, either from Ted's stories at work or an occasional meeting. At the stores that we frequently shopped at, clerks became familiar with Amanda. There was not another tiny blonde girl in a petite wheelchair to compare her to. And Amanda was cute, so everyone said hi to her or offered to lend a hand if it looked like she needed help.

We were a busy family, too. Kristen and Jillian kept us running to dance classes, soccer games, and school functions. As a family, we went to the movies, the mall, the skating rink, and church picnics. People only had to meet Amanda once, and they would never forget her. So we could randomly run into a seeming stranger, who would invariably look at Amanda and exclaim, "I remember you!" We'd then get reminded of our one chance meeting a year or more ago, where their memory took a permanent snapshot of Amanda.

Unlike Kristen and Jillian, whose friends remained pretty much permanent and present throughout the school years, Amanda's special-needs friends came in and out of the picture all the time. They remembered us, and we'd remember them. When Lyle died, I don't know how much Amanda understood about his passing. I don't remember talking a whole bunch about it to her. In Amanda's head, he was just gone for a while. Through the years, if I would hear of the passing of one of Amanda's special friends, I would not even tell Amanda about it. It scared the hell out of me. It brought the reality of death too close to our home. Amanda had plenty of friends to run into, and I did not want her to consider why we weren't running into a few others.

19
Special School vs. Local School

Amanda continued in the POHI program through first grade, when I began to question her schooling and the challenges it presented. First of all, the school was several cities away, and it was not convenient to go get Amanda from school when they would call for me to pick her up. From her younger days of frequent vomiting due to plugged shunts, Amanda had a sensitive gag reflex that had her easily choking on a small bit of lunch and puking. I'd be called to pick her up from school, either because they thought she had the flu or because her clothes were too puked upon to salvage. Or she would have a stinky accident in her pants that would be too extreme for the paraprofessionals to clean up. Some days I think Amanda claimed a headache or stomach ache just to have Mom bring her home early. It was particularly challenging to this mom, because going to pick her up meant

PASS IT ON

A paraprofessional, or special-education aide, will work in support of your child's teacher in the classroom to implement the best education plan for your child.

loading up a toddler and a baby to make the drive to Taylor.

By the time Amanda was in first grade, I also had Kristen in a local preschool, so schedules started conflicting. I started noticing a real difference in the atmosphere of the school Amanda was attending and the elementary school near our home in Trenton. The Taylor School was very loud! As a whole, the Trenton Elementary School felt more calm, controlled, and quiet. I felt the loud noise and chaos at the Taylor School was stressful for Amanda. Maybe that was another reason for her calls to me to come get her. The other issue was that Amanda was making some friends who were not in her own neighborhood. That made after-school playdates and friendships darn near impossible. The other thing that was happening in our area in the late 1980s was the concept of "mainstreaming" special-education students.

PASS IT ON

Mainstreaming is wonderful. To have special-needs children attend school in the same neighborhood where they live and where siblings attend makes them feel like part of the family. It also encourages the community to become comfortable with a member who is different.

Instead of sending off the broken kids to special schools, the thought was to include them in their own local schools. It probably made transportation issues easier for everyone, as well as making the special student feel included with the rest of the "normal" kids and enabling him or her to make neighborhood friendships.

After she completed preschool, kindergarten, and first grade in Taylor, we transferred Amanda to the elementary school near our house. It ended up being a wonderful change. At that time, Amanda's younger sister Kristen was also at the local school, with Jillian joining them in another year or two. It felt like "home" to have all three daughters in the same school.

The elementary years were revealing. With each passing year, it became more and more obvious that Amanda just couldn't grasp and learn a lot of what was being taught. I dreaded whatever homework she brought home, knowing I'd be sitting with her at the kitchen table for hours while I helped her through it. I also dreaded report-card time. Amanda's sisters brought home report cards with mostly As and Bs. Amanda's report cards liked to journey a little farther into the alphabet and included Cs and Ds. I kept hoping that a switch in her brain would click and the learning engine would start working. But each report card brought grades a little lower than the last. For many years I hoped for Amanda to get good grades, until it just hurt too much to expect them anymore. I tried to focus on the areas where grades were good. She was good at spelling. Strangely, she had a knack for memorizing things like how to spell words and even remembering phone numbers. But math was like a foreign language to her. And although Amanda could read words and sentences, to comprehend and correctly answer questions about the material she just read was not possible. Eventually, I stopped hoping for any good grades and was anxious for her to do well enough simply to pass each grade. So she spent time with special tutors for kids with learning problems.

Meanwhile, I had two other daughters following behind her who were breezing through school and homework. In fact, they took part in a talented and gifted program. Two normal, bright daughters, and another one who was struggling with everything set before her. The two extremes had me often feeling like a knot in the middle of a tug-of-war.

Jillian, Kristen, and Amanda, 1990.

20
More Surgery

If I could keep everyone where they belonged and doing what they should be doing, life was good. Through the years, there were science projects and field trips, dance and art classes, birthday sleepovers and holiday parties. However, there was always this sort of "menace" hovering in the wings, offstage from this pretty family picture. The best way I have come to describe it is this: you see, we have this dragon in our lives. Now, everyone knows that dragons don't exist and are mythical creatures. No one has seen a dragon. But we really do have one. Its name is either "surgery" or "sickness." Most of the time, I don't see or feel our dragon, and life is pleasant and safe. But sometimes Amanda would get sick, or I'd hear the doctors talk about some necessary surgery that would need scheduling. Just

> **THE HELPING HAND**
>
> *Life with a handicapped child is stressful. Even when things are running smoothly, another surgery may be looming on the horizon. We try not to let the worry consume us, but please excuse our anxiety as we tend to live on the edge.*

when things were going so well and I'd forget that this dragon existed, I would feel its fiery breath on the back of my neck. Or Amanda would get sick and we'd know that something was just not right, and I was sure I could feel the pulsing, whooshing beat of the dragon's wings as panic would set in.

Another surgery would disrupt the whole family, and it would feel like an uninvited guest, our dragon, was back. For the family at home, this meant that Mom would be gone, since I stayed with Amanda during her hospitalizations. Ted willingly arranged his work schedule to take over more mom duties each time. Kristen and Jillian survived just fine, but there is no comparison to having Mom make breakfast, pack your school lunch, or French-braid your hair for the day. If there were a school assembly or soccer game to play, the girls had to accept that only one parent would be there. Ted did wonderfully each time, filling in as best he could while working full-time, but the bills and the laundry piled up while the fridge emptied and the house cluttered. It was as if the smoke left from the dragon's fire had blanketed our family's normal routine as chaos slowly tried to filter in. If I could have done something to appease the dragon to keep it away, I would have. I would have done anything.

I recently asked Kristen and Jillian about their childhood recollections of growing up with Amanda and what it was like with her being in the hospital so much. Jillian reflected that the majority of Amanda's surgeries were before Amanda was even ten years old. And since Jill was four years younger than Amanda, she didn't really remember most of them. Jillian never really felt that it was any big deal for Amanda to be going to the hospital, because it was all Jill had ever known. For Jillian, it was normal to have her older sister hospitalized from time to time. Older Kristen, however, was another case. She didn't remember being overly concerned about Amanda having to go to the hospital; it was just part of our lives. She did remember it being a nuisance when her life got all out of sync. She told me that she hated when Ted's folks came to stay at the house during Amanda's hospitalizations. It wasn't because she didn't like her grandparents, but they weren't familiar with the day-to-day routine of breakfast and school, curfews and house rules. Life just got topsy-turvy, and the family normal was disrupted.

I've often been asked the number of surgeries that Amanda has had, and I honestly do not know the answer. Each one was unwelcome and uncomfortable. I did not write it down and keep track. We were trying so hard to raise our daughters in a happy and healthy home. When the dragon loomed and we found ourselves with Amanda in the hospital again, we simply dealt with this unwelcome guest and got through it. I think there were at least twenty surgeries.

As I've already described, Amanda had one shunt surgery every month or so in her first year. That accounts for about ten surgeries right there. There were at least three more shunt surgeries in her elementary years—once or twice when it got plugged up, and another time or two they had to put in new tubing. Because Amanda was getting bigger, her tubing had to be made longer to keep up with her growth.

Surgery and doctors' visits were a normal part of Amanda's life. She never questioned it. By this time, our nonverbal Amanda had become quite a chatterbox. Her chatter did not include the why's of her extensive medical care, either because it was all she'd known since birth or else she cognitively was not capable of such a discussion. Since she was just a child, she simply went where I took her, whether it was to the store or to the doctor's. She did not like the medical visits and let us know early on by her fearful crying that the people in white coats were not her preference. If there was an upcoming scheduled surgery, she might ask how long she would be in the hospital. If it was an unscheduled shunt surgery, she was usually feeling too sick to ask questions. After surgery, her conversation would be about what she was going to choose to eat from the yucky hospital menu or when she was going home, or she would engage a doctor or nurse in friendly, shallow chitchat about day-to-day things.

Shunt surgeries paved the way for other neurological problems for Amanda. The "domino effect" of already having hydrocephalus simply resulted in other breakdowns in normal neurological function. Sometimes spina bifida kids have a condition called "tethered cord." If you remember from my earlier description, there is a break in the vertebrae of spina bifida kids that disrupts and injures the fragile nerves running through the spinal column. Amanda had surgery when she was a day old to close up the hole in her back. As with any surgery, scar tissue formed, and it can be sticky stuff. With tethered cord, the contents of the spinal column get stuck in places to scar tissue. So Amanda had surgery to fix that problem.

PASS IT ON

Arnold-Chiari malformation is named after two pathologists from the early 1900s who identified this condition, characterized by a compression deformity of the lower brain.

Going hand in hand with tethered cord, she also had to have surgery to correct an Arnold-Chiari malformation. With Arnold-Chiari, the base of the brain gets pulled down, and it compresses as it tries to fit down into the canal through the upper vertebrae. It puts a lot of pressure on functions of the brain stem. This was not a pleasant surgery. It involved cutting vertically along the back of Amanda's neck. I'm not sure how or what the surgeons do to fix things, but it has to do with grinding away the inside of the neck bones to open up the narrow space, which results in making room for everything and, thus, alleviating brain parts being squished.

I was absolutely terrified after this surgery, thinking the doctors had totally chopped Amanda's brain to pieces. Amanda generally bounced back quickly after a surgery, but this time she was not bouncing. She was very disoriented and illogical. I kept telling the nurses that she just wasn't acting right. During her recovery in the hospital, Amanda was mostly sleeping, and when she did talk, she was fuzzy and distant. Usually, once anesthetic wore off, Amanda could always tell me if she were in pain or what food she wanted to choose from her hospital menu. I was a wreck and kept crying. At one point, Amanda was sleeping on her stomach and had an intravenous line in her hand, with a plastic board taped under it to keep her hand stretched out for the IV. She woke up for a few minutes, and thinking the plastic board was a book, kept saying, "Here, Mom, take this book," as she tried to pass the plastic board to me. I kept thinking, all those years and years of work to get Amanda to read and talk and make all the progress she had, were now ruined.

After several days of this, I was exhausted with grief. Finally, she snapped out of it, and we had our old Amanda back. The only explanation for this bizarre behavior we could find was that the combination of her brain being somewhat swollen from surgery and the pain drugs she was on had made her loopy. Once the brain settled down and recovered from surgical invasion and the pain medications were withdrawn, things eventually healed and returned to normal. It sure was a scary trip, though.

21
Growing and More "How-to-Go" Issues

As if neurological issues weren't enough, Amanda's incontinence continued to give us challenges. For me, catheterizing Amanda was simple, but not at all convenient. You basically "put the straw in the hole." Since Amanda has no sensation from about the waist on down, the whole process never really bothered her because she could never feel it. And Amanda didn't really care who cathed her, either. Having grown up under the

---
PASS IT ON

A quick Internet search will provide a wealth of resources for adaptive clothing to help with various toileting and dressing challenges.

constant scrutiny of doctors and nurses, as well as depending on others for most of her physical care, Amanda was not one to feel any modesty.

There were only two ways to cath her. The easiest was to lay her down on the bed or couch, and we'd cath her into her own little plastic pee pot. This, of course, didn't work if you were out to eat, or at the mall, or anywhere but home. The second way was to have Amanda scooch her hips forward to the edge of her wheelchair seat, and after getting all the clothing out of the way, you hoped to find your target.

Going pee at school proved to be a fun challenge for the paraprofessionals. To make it easier for them, Amanda would wear dresses to school or pants that were altered to open at the side seams, usually by Velcro, so that you could pull the whole front down. As I stated before, getting around to places with someone in a wheelchair is easy. Most places are handicapped-accessible these days. The incontinence issues are, by far, the greater challenge. They pose so many questions. Who was going to cath her? When was she going to need to be cath'd? Did she have all the necessary supplies in her backpack? What if there were no bathrooms big enough for her wheelchair? What if we were at someone's house and their bathroom wasn't large enough? What if she didn't get cath'd in time and her bladder let loose its load? Did we have spare dry clothes packed, and what to do about the wet wheelchair seat? Who could we get to take care of Amanda's bladder-relieving issues so we could go away for a night?

Bowel issues were just as much fun. As the years went on, we achieved the best success with a "bowel cleansing" program. It worked by, basically, giving Amanda an enema every other day and then just sitting her on the potty for thirty minutes. Flush out the bowels, and flush it all away! Accidents happened occasionally, but it worked. Every other night was the routine, and it at least made for some nights where we didn't have to spend all that time in the bathroom. But, between the bowel issue and the cathing, pooping and peeing was far from a normal process for Amanda, and kept us busy as her primary, and only, caregivers. She was just a bit more than the normal babysitter could handle. A lot more actually.

There was our favorite high school babysitter, whom I will call Lisa. Lisa was very mature and was wonderful when babysitting for all three of my girls. There was a time coming up when Ted and I were trying to be gone for an overnight, and I thought that Lisa would have no problems learning how to cath Amanda. I was hoping to show her how and let Lisa spend one night at our house with our daughters. When I excitedly related to Lisa's mom my plan

THE HELPING HAND

Many tasks that caregivers perform daily are not normal or comfortable tasks for the general population. Caregivers must strive to keep that in perspective. Family and friends might try to step out of their comfort zones.

to utilize her very responsible and lovely daughter Lisa for an overnight of babysitting, including cathing Amanda, I was immediately met with a no. There was no way her daughter Lisa was going to cath Amanda! I didn't even get to ask Lisa, and I'm pretty confident she would have said yes and it would have been no big deal. But Lisa's mom had issues with the cathing and gave her final no on the issue. Lisa could have and would have done it. In hindsight, now that I am older and wiser, I realize that perhaps I was wrong in expecting Lisa to perform such a foreign task as cathing Amanda. For Ted and me, it was part of our normal day-to-day routine. It was not normal for your typical babysitter.

THE HELPING HAND

Parents and caregivers definitely need a break from time to time. In hindsight, the effort it took for a night away from our children was well worth it. Never give up in finding ways to get away. Even a couple-hour break can be a sanity restorer.

Every night out and away from our children proved to be challenging. We first had to find a sitter who wasn't intimidated by a child in a wheelchair. Second, the sitter had to be willing to keep up with three little girls. In addition, Amanda's sensitive gag reflex scared off many a sitter who could not deal with an Amanda puke episode. Even if the evening went off smoothly for the kids and sitter, Ted and I still could not come home from a night out to relax. One of us would have to go wake Amanda to cath her. The sitter couldn't cath her, and it really had to be done at bedtime if we didn't want Amanda to wake up to a wet bed.

22
Amanda's Uniqueness: Strange Quirks

Despite her physical challenges, Amanda has compensated for her inabilities with a personality that is full of both puzzling complexities and humor. Amanda had a time, like most young children, when Santa Claus was terrifying to her. She eventually outgrew her fear of the fat red guy and actually enjoyed sitting on his lap each Christmas. This would not be the same case for other costumed characters.

No matter how many times we'd explain to Amanda that it was simply a costume with a real person underneath, the sighting of a costumed character would instill instant panic. Over the years, there were many times that we would take the girls to an Easter egg hunt. Amanda would spy the costumed Easter egg character and literally start puking in fear. Another time, Amanda went cheerfully on the school bus to an excitedly

PASS IT ON

Leporiphobia is the fear of rabbits. Coulrophobia is the fear of clowns. There is no word to describe a specific fear of the Easter bunny or of costumed people.

121

anticipated Halloween day of school, but when the bus pulled into the school parking lot and Amanda looked out at the costumed people, she threw up and I got the call to come bring "sick" Amanda home. Years of puking at costumed characters, with follow-up lectures to explain how the characters were simply real, normal people in fabric and plastic constructed attire, could never convince her to give up her fear.

Amanda's best gift, which has helped her most along the way, is how very sociable she is. I believe a lot of this ability comes from all the hours she spent in the hospital when she was younger. For all the times spent waiting to see doctors and hours passed in a hospital room, she has learned to talk to every stranger who shows up. Engaging in a conversation can cure boredom, as well as delay the unpleasant poke or test that is about to happen. Amanda learned that she could distract the doctor if she could snatch him up in a conversation. People, for the most part, would also show patience and compassion while Amanda spoke to them. They didn't want to be mean or rude to the poor sweet little girl in the wheelchair. Watching from the side as Amanda would engage in conversation with someone, I would marvel at how Amanda could keep her listener captured to the point that he or she would start looking at a watch and wonder how to end the conversation politely so he or she could get away. You could say that Amanda has the gift of gab. For those with time and patience, she will talk with you for hours. This gift makes her invaluable as a nursing home visitor. Amanda makes the perfect companion for a senior citizen with plenty of time and words on their hands.

Amanda's humorous side shines through at times when she just suddenly says the darndest things. I remember one hot summer day when the girls were all little. It had been a typical morning of busy little girls. By lunchtime, I think my patience was wearing thin from the toys, clutter, demands, and noise of three little girls in a sticky, hot house that did not have air-conditioning. I can't recall exactly what happened that finally made me snap, but it ended with a potted plant that was on the windowsill next to the lunch table taking a tumble to the floor. In anger and frustration, I raised my voice and yelled, causing the two younger ones to flee the kitchen to the safer realm of their rooms. Amanda could not leave because she was sitting in one of those hook-to-the-table booster seats. I had lost control and was on my hands and knees, cleaning up the spilled dirt on the floor with tears streaming down my face. Amanda continued to calmly and quietly eat her lunch. After a few minutes of watching me, Amanda smiled and said to me in her squeaky, high-pitched voice, "Mom, you look like Cinderella!" Her comment turned my crying into laughter. All my anger dissipated into giggles. I've never forgotten that incident. And I've been brought back to that memory many times over the years when I have felt like Cinderella.

Being a mom is sort of like being a Cinderella. Don't moms always handle the dirty work when the house is full of small children? There's the laundry, the dishes, the diaper changes, the bathing of children, the dusting, and the scrubbing of floors and toilets. Moms also take care to see that the children are dressed nicely, with smudges wiped off hands and faces clean so that they can go presentably to school or church. We clean up the messes and take care of our children—often before we get ourselves ready. Just like Cinderella had to tend first to the needs and demands of her stepmother and stepsisters. If Cinderella was lucky, she had time for herself and even got to go (once) to a ball! As our children grow, they take over the tasks of cleaning up and getting themselves washed and dressed so we can become less like poor Cinderella. I've been tending to Amanda for over twenty-nine years now. Cinderella is getting old and tired. I hope I make it to the ball someday.

Amanda, Kristen, and Jillian, 1991.

23
Farewell to Another Friend

For a short time in her early elementary school years, Amanda was involved with an athletic group for disabled people in the area. They had a wheelchair basketball team, as well as young people in the group who ran track or played softball. Those sports were of no interest to Amanda, but she did participate in their bowling team. On this team was a girl named Kalie. Kalie had challenges very similar to Amanda's. Kalie did not have spina bifida, but had challenges resulting from an auto accident. I can't recall if she was hit by a car or was in a car that was involved in an accident. However, she must have suffered some sort of spinal injury, which left her a paraplegic. Kalie had to cath herself, and because she could not use her legs, was also mobile by means of a wheelchair. The one thing she had that was different from Amanda was a tracheotomy. Apparently, she had some challenges with her breathing and needed assistance at times. Kalie had a lot of upper body

> **WHISPERS FROM GOD**
>
> Ecclesiastes 3:4 *A time to weep and a time to laugh; a time to mourn and a time to dance.*

strength and was always scooting quickly around the bowling alley in her wheelchair. She could cath herself and would disappear into the bathroom to take care of that task, which I found to be quite amazing as I wished Amanda could handle that task on her own. Kalie always seemed strong, able, confident, healthy, and independent to me. Being a few years older than my Amanda, she was the perfect role model for Amanda.

A year or so after Amanda's last bowling with Kalie, I came across her obituary. Kalie had died. I couldn't believe it. If you had taken a moment to quickly compare Amanda with Kalie, it was easy to see who the stronger one was. I don't know what her cause of death was. I just know I was shocked and saddened. I told Ted, but I didn't tell Amanda. Amanda had not seen Kalie in probably a year or more, so there were no current memories to create a feeling of loss. And like other times, the sting of death was felt too painfully close to home, and I was afraid to bring it up with Amanda.

24
Mom Grows Up and Heads Off to College: Amanda Stops Growing

It was somewhere around 1991, and life was on a temporary even keel. I say "temporary" because I never knew when the winds would change or the dragon would loom. But life must have been steady enough, because I had the chance to think beyond the needs of my children. Like most good moms, I always put the needs of my young children first. But with all the years of caregiving I had now logged in tending to Amanda's needs, as well as the hospital hours I'd put in, I began to think that a nursing career would be an easy goal for me. Perhaps I also needed to turn a little attention to myself at this time. When I spoke to Ted about my becoming a nurse, he was very supportive. He knew I needed a diversion outside of being a mom and homemaker, and quickly supported my decision to return to school. I managed to get previous transcripts sent to the local college and got myself accepted. There were still several prerequisites that I needed to take, but thus began the process of getting into nursing school. One college class a semester seemed easy enough at this time, and the academic challenges were a welcome diversion to my otherwise life of full-time motherhood.

Despite being a high school honor student and now taking college classes, I often found myself challenged in trying to figure out some of Amanda's far-from-normal behaviors, as well as so many medical mysteries that have stumped us through the years. Although this wasn't directly the catalyst for my going to nursing school, I was sure I could become an even better "nurse" to Amanda than the already-great one I was. Through the years, I had picked up gobs of information and education about medical stuff just from listening to the doctors around me and Amanda. I could take care of Amanda better than anyone and was also performing plenty of nurse-ish things. After all, I could catheterize and do bandage changes. And I could even sound medically smart when I spoke to the doctors, using much of the medical terms and lingo I'd heard them speaking.

Probably the first big mystery about Amanda was: why did she never grow? Stunted growth was not a typical occurrence with spina bifida patients. As a baby, she was not keeping up on the growth charts, so I was advised to bulk up her bottle feedings. So I had a plump Amanda who was putting on weight, but not gaining any proportional length. I must say she was the cutest little thing when she put on that fat baby weight and started looking like a roly-poly Buddha baby. Once the nurses and doctors at the clinic realized that Amanda was getting too heavy, the advice changed to instead water down her bottle feedings. I felt horrible feeding my baby such a watered-down formula, but we lost the Buddha baby look, although we still did not gain any growth in height.

As we approached the later elementary school years, we decided to consult an endocrinologist to investigate why she wasn't growing. But at nine years old, Amanda's growth issues were further complicated by back problems. As is typical for spina bifida patients, the spine ended up growing in an "S" shape. Known as scoliosis, Amanda's backbone started growing incorrectly. Instead of growing straight and long, it grew sideways in one direction and then another, putting her spine in the shape of a compressed "S." Amanda's curved back was causing her to collapse in the middle, putting pressure on her lungs and intestines. The intestines don't work as well if they are all squished, and breathing can become quite labored if the lungs cannot expand. The solution? Surgery, of course. The doctors would straighten her curved spine as straight as they could and insert metal rods along her backbone to permanently fuse everything straight. Talk of straightening and fusing her twisting spine was happening concurrently with discussions of perhaps trying growth hormone to get her to grow taller.

I was devastated when considering that Amanda was going to remain so tiny. I believe I was still caught up subconsciously thinking that I wanted Amanda to be normal, to grow normally. As a temporary fix in the months leading up to this surgery, she was forced to wear a plastic clamshell kind of brace. While she lay on the floor, we would slide the back shell underneath her, and then the front part of the clamshell-like brace was fitted on her topside. Velcro straps pulled the whole thing together as it pushed her compressed sides in, thus elongating her torso and forcing her spine to stretch as straight as possible. The doctors were hoping we could forcibly train her spine to grow straight, while at the same time opening up her chest cavity so she could breathe more easily. Amanda did not like being strapped into this thing. It was hot and very difficult to move in.

The scoliosis issue won, and we were forced into having her spine fused before her middle collapsed anymore. Spinal fusion meant that Amanda would not be able to have any more torso growth. Surgery would fuse and fix her back permanently. Amanda didn't question why she was having another surgery, but accepted our explanation of how straightening her back would help her. All we had to do was tell Amanda that she could toss her back brace and never wear it again after back surgery, and she was a happy little girl. The growth hormone idea and any further treatment to help with growth were abandoned.

Amanda, Laurel, Kristen, and Jillian, 1992.

25
The Most Terrifying Surgery of All

It was 1992, and the dragon breathed fire as he swooped down for a most frightening visit. Back surgery loomed on the horizon as the scariest surgery of them all. To straighten a curved back, the spine is pulled as straight as possible and then wired for support and stability to metal rods. The surgery to insert rods is pretty wicked. Amanda would first be opened up on her front side, and they would reach through to her spine, do some work, and then close her up. Next, they would flip her over and slice open from neck to tailbone and finish the job, inserting rods and screws.

We had several months to get through before Amanda's surgery date. I was an emotional wreck for the whole time. She needed the surgery. But it was such a long, extensive surgery. I knew the whole family would be sad as we separated into our two halves: those at the hospital and those at home. I was scared for Amanda going through such a radical surgery, and I dreaded the hospitalization time and the recovery I would have to nurse Amanda through afterward.

This surgery didn't involve simply a hand or a foot. It wasn't just another shunt surgery, either. This was major surgery, with lots of long incisions, lots of time on the operating table, and working around all major body organs. I was positively petrified that this might be the surgery that Amanda wasn't going to live through. Just thinking about it made my eyes well up with tears. If I were driving around town and happened to go past the local funeral home, my heart would suddenly beat faster and harder as I tried to avoid panic. I would purposely turn my head away from the funeral home and refuse to look at it.

I was so scared that I would be planning a funeral for Amanda. Of course, trying *not* to think of something makes it inevitable that you *will* think of it. Disney's movie *Aladdin* had been out for a while, and I kept hearing the song "A Whole New World" from the movie, being played over and over on the radio. In the movie, the princess is trapped in her strict and secure lifestyle in the palace, with little freedom to go beyond the safe walls to explore the world. As she escapes to take a magic carpet ride, the song describes the thrilling sights, indescribable feelings, and unleashed thrill and joy of soaring above and beyond anywhere she had been before. I thought it would be the perfect song for Amanda's funeral.

I had visions of Amanda passing away and having this wonderful angel taking her to heaven. It would be her magic carpet ride! And Princess Amanda would soar above the clouds and finally be whole. She would see things in a whole new clarity! She would be able to do things that she never could before. With the wind in her hair and excitement on her face, she would thrill at her whole new world. Released from the bondage of her broken earthly body, she would be given one awesome ride and tour of everything from a new heavenly perspective. I would imagine Amanda strong, pink, and healthy—and joyously happy. No more surgeries, pain, restrictions, or barriers. Darned if I didn't cry every time that song came on the radio.

I had my own heaven-sent message in the months leading up to Amanda's back surgery. Larry and Bertha Manning had been dear neighbors of ours. They were an elderly couple with grown children and grandchildren. My daughters would always find their way into Larry and Bertha's backyard when outside playing. My girls called Bertha "Grandma Bertha," and she was always so patient and kind to the girls. Whatever Grandma Bertha was doing, she'd let the girls be part of it. Whether it was sharing a pitcher of lemonade on the back patio or helping Grandma Bertha snap her green beans for dinner that night, she welcomed the girls as her own granddaughters.

Larry was always working on something in the garage or out in the yard. He affectionately teased the girls and would always take the time to explain to them about the project he was currently working on. Larry ended up dying from cancer, and Grandma Bertha moved to a smaller apartment, something easier for her to take care of than the house and yard she had shared with her husband. Because she had moved away, we didn't get to see Grandma Bertha anymore, and in the months preceding Amanda's back surgery, we had new neighbors.

One night, as I tried to lose myself to sleep away from the worries of Amanda's upcoming surgery, Larry came to me in a dream. In my dream, I was walking in our backyard when Larry appeared from between the shrubs that ran like a dotted line between our backyard and Larry's driveway. In my dream, I knew that Larry had died and was surprised to see him alive and still walking on this earth. He walked up to me and stopped to speak. With his face full of love, care, and compassion, he looked me in the eye and said, "Don't you worry about your little girl Amanda. If she doesn't make it through her surgery, I'll be here to help her find her way." That was the end of my dream, and I woke up and sobbed. It was so very real.

I know, from the bottom of my heart, that Larry somehow knew from his home in heaven that I was worried. I'm sure God knew of my worries—hadn't I been pouring out my heart and soul to Him in prayer for weeks? In hindsight, I'm sure God was trying to teach me to trust in Him. I'm sure He wanted me to know that He heard my prayers and knew of my pain and agony in worrying about losing Amanda. I can picture Him calling His faithful servant Larry over to His side and them talking about us. I know without a doubt that God sent Larry to me in a dream to give me a message. God could have simply come and told me that everything was going to be all right, but I think he didn't do that because He wanted me to trust Him for whatever outcome there was going to be. Besides, God tells us all the time in His Word not to worry about tomorrow.

WHISPERS FROM GOD

Psalm 34:4 *I sought the Lord, and He heard me, And delivered me from all my fears.*

I wish I could find my "worry switch" and turn it off like He wants me to! But I haven't figured out how to do that yet! God simply sent his servant Larry to assure me that Amanda would find her way to heaven if she couldn't survive the surgery. And there were people who knew and loved her to help her find her way. I cry every time I relate this dream to others because I feel it is the closest taste I've had of heaven. To have Larry deliver this message to me meant that God heard my prayers of fear. My prayers really were heard. The dream was so real, so pure, and so full of love and passion. I felt humbled at being the recipient of such a message. I was amazed that God would take the time to hear my pleas and let Larry be my angel messenger. This big balloon of emotions swells up inside of me as I feel the love and power of our great Lord, who hears our prayers from heaven. And I feel it all, I relive the dream, I know He is real, and the tears fall.

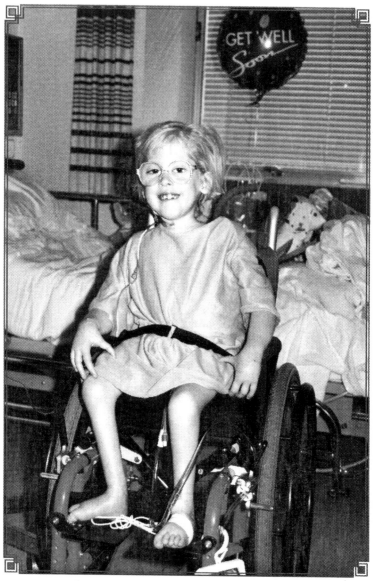

*Amanda sitting up in her wheelchair for the first time
after her back surgery.*

26
A Surgical Fix for Bathroom Needs

Obviously, Amanda made it through her back surgery. Now with metal rods wired to her spine, Amanda sat taller, straighter, and with much more stability. One negative from this surgery was the fact that in terms of her growing anymore in trunk length, she was done. The rods froze her nine-year-old body into the size it was. Her arms and legs might grow a little more in length, but her torso would not. In a way, though, Amanda's "smallness" has been a blessing. All too often, wheelchair-dependent individuals can easily take in more calories than they burn, resulting in obesity. The extra weight can make it more difficult for the handicapped person to get around and leads to other potential health issues. The extra weight also provides extra challenges for the caregiver. Amanda weighs in around forty-five pounds and is about forty-some inches long. I can't measure how tall she is, since she hasn't stood up since her parapodium and walking braces days. With Amanda lying down and somewhat stretched out, she measures somewhere around forty inches. Having cared for Amanda for twenty-nine years, I can tell you that my joints ache from the strain. I can't imagine what my joints would feel like if Amanda had been one hundred pounds or more. I would much rather have to lift a forty-five-pound Amanda than a one-hundred-and-forty-five-pound Amanda. Back-straightening surgery would forever keep Amanda small, but her lighter weight would benefit both her and her caregivers. It was a trade-off. .

A year or so after back surgery, Amanda faced more major surgery. This time it was bowel and bladder issues. Incontinence continued to pose challenges, and our best hopes for Amanda's bowel and bladder issues came from Dr. Gonzales. Dr. Gonzales was a urologist who became part of the team of doctors who saw patients like Amanda at the clinic in Children's Hospital in Detroit. He had worked previously with adult patients who were wheelchair-bound and seeking a better quality of life. Let's face it, requiring someone to help you get your pants off to get a catheter or enema in you is not exactly a fun and friendly social interaction. There's a little embarrassment, not to mention a loss of dignity. Amanda was fairly comfortable with people always helping her go to the bathroom. Although embarrassment was not so great an issue, it was a great deal to her parents if we could change things for Amanda so that she was exposed as little as possible—especially since Amanda depended on other people to help cath her when Ted and I were not around. It would also be nice if the whole cathing thing were a little bit easier to perform. Maybe even something Amanda could do herself.

Dr. Gonzales proposed a surgery for Amanda. He would connect her bladder to her belly button so that we could insert a catheter into her belly button, a natural indented hole, and it would thread through to her bladder. This surgical procedure had already been a godsend for many paraplegic adults who had, perhaps, struggled with the fine motor skill of cathing themselves and had found this to be a much easier task to accomplish. The target was much more obvious and accessible. If they needed assistance with the cathing, patient dignity was maintained. The beauty of it was that Amanda could have a caregiver cath her without ever taking her pants off. The surgical

THE HELPING HAND

Never stop searching for a solution to caregiving challenges. Techniques of care and surgical solutions are constantly evolving.

procedure is called a "Mitrofanoff," as it is named after the French surgeon who developed it in 1980, Dr. Paul Mitrofanoff.

Along with the Mitrofanoff, Dr. Gonzales also suggested the MACE procedure for bowel management. This procedure involved creating access on Amanda's abdomen to her large intestine. This was in no way similar to a colostomy, in which bowel contents spill out into a collection bag that is stuck by adhesive to the skin. The small hole would be made about an inch or two next to Amanda's belly button. It would provide access to the ascending, or starting part, of Amanda's large intestine. Through a catheter inserted in this hole, we could instill an enema that would help flush everything through the large intestine and, well, out the end. Like the Mitrofanoff, this hole did not leak to the outside. When the holes are not in use, they look like a normal belly button and a small pink bump.

In our house, every other night is a "poop night," and we sit Amanda on the potty and flush her with an enema to clean out the poop! Gross as it sounds, that's life. And pooping is important, because not pooping has its own problems over time, and we don't want to go there! The beauty of the MACE, like the Mitrofanoff, is the easy access, which makes it fairly simple for the caregiver to instill the enema. This surgery was much easier to endure, as it didn't involve messing with spinal cords and nerves, lung and breathing issues, or huge, open incisions. Postoperatively, there was little pain, as most of the work was done below belly button level, so Amanda felt no discomfort. There were lots of tubes placed everywhere that had to stay put until things healed, but that was only a temporary inconvenience. Healing and recovery went unchallenged. Incontinence would always be an issue for Amanda, but we could now deal with it in the best uncomplicated way known to current, modern medicine.

PASS IT ON

The MACE procedure, or the Malone Antegrade Continence Enema, has been around for twenty years.

Cathing was much easier now. Just getting at the target, her belly button, was a breeze. No longer did she have to wear dresses or pants that opened on the sides to school anymore. There were more options for clothes for Amanda now. And she stayed warmer on cold days because she didn't have to get half undressed to be cathed. It was easier to teach a friend or paraprofessional how to cath Amanda. Amanda would smile and lift her shirt, exposing her belly button, and tell people to stick the catheter in that belly button hole. Her belly button looked like just any old belly button, yet you could stick a catheter into it and it slid almost all the way in. It was kind of a novel thing and made the potential embarrassment of the person being taught to cath dissolve into navel humor.

Life with a wheelchair-driven Amanda really revolves around her toileting schedule. The poop and pee issues make her more handicapped than her wheelchair does. Every day I have to think ahead as to where I will be when it's time to cath. If I don't cath in time, her overexpanded bladder will finally take the strain no more and Amanda will wet from the bottom, leaving me with her wet clothes and wheelchair to clean up and change. If I will be gone all day, I have to plan for someone to come to the house and cath her. If I leave for the day and take Amanda with me, I have to pack cathing supplies and think ahead as to where I'll be, in hopes of there being a clean and accessible bathroom. On the rare occasion that Ted and I can be gone somewhere overnight without Amanda, I have to pay generously for a trained friend or babysitter to spend the night. The cathing part is fairly simple, and I have used college-age friends over the years to spend a night or two. All the work is done with a clothed Amanda sitting in front of you with, simply, her shirt pulled up a little to expose her belly button. The pooping issue is a bit more complicated. Amanda has to be picked up and placed on the potty. It gets stinky, and then there's the wipe up afterward. No one has volunteered for this job.

The longest Ted and I have been away for most of twenty-nine years is two nights. We always have to get back because Amanda needs to poop. People have asked me why I don't use respite care services. The answer is I'm scared. The respite care service people would need training and, well, I don't know them. Would you allow a stranger to stick tubes in your child and help him or her on and off the potty? We have always used someone we knew, and yet we have never conquered teaching them the pooping part of Amanda's care. And I have no family who have offered to help, either.

What I would give for a carefree week of vacation with just Ted and me.

Jillian, Kristen, and Amanda, 1993.

27
Heaven Claims Another Friend

With the frightening back surgery behind us and bowel and bladder issues being handled as efficiently as possible now thanks to surgery, the Greshels were all making fair progress. It was 1995, and Amanda, Kristen, and Jillian were twelve, ten, and eight years old. Life revolved around home, friends, church, family, and school. As the girls had grown and completed several grades in school, I too accomplished my educational goal. The spring of 1995, I graduated from nursing school. In hindsight, I don't know how I did it in the midst of taking care of house and home while weathering several large surgeries with Amanda, but I did. Thanks to my dear husband, who was always so supportive and encouraging through the years to help with the girls and home when I couldn't. He never complained and was always there to pick up the slack.

We were finally at a point in Amanda's life where the days and weeks were no longer measured and remembered by doctor appointments, therapy sessions, and surgeries. With all the major physical issues behind us, we could focus on education and learning life skills. Of course, our fearsome dragon always loomed in the shadows, where he waited to pounce on us and breathe fire when we least suspected. But for the time being, the dragon kept himself at bay while our only doctor visits were for sore throats or yearly checkups.

About once a year, Amanda had to be seen at the Children's Hospital of Michigan myelo clinic. It was the once-a-year checkup where Amanda waited around all day in an exam room while all her doctors took their turn to see her. It was always a very long and tiring day. While sitting in the reception area on one such clinic day, we were completing all the necessary registration paperwork when who should we meet up with but our sweet little red-haired friend Marleena! It was good to see her after so many years. There had been many after-school playdates for Amanda and Marleena. Several times her parents brought her to our house in Trenton for them to play. Many times, Marleena's mom would walk the two girls home from school in Taylor to her house. They lived near the school, and while Marleena could walk, Amanda would get pushed by Marleena's mom. I would come by later to pick Amanda up. The girls had even spent a week together while at camp for two summers when they were younger.

The girls were now entering their teens. Apparently Marleena had not been doing well and was in for a checkup. She had been experiencing many shunt problems and had been in and out of the hospital a lot. She had also put on quite a lot of weight and could no longer walk like she did before, opting for a wheelchair to get around. We spoke briefly with her. The shunt problems had taken a toll on Marleena. The spunky, energetic, red-haired little girl I remembered was gone. I couldn't believe it. Marleena used to walk and had been so full of life. There was barely a flicker left of what was once a bright and glowing Marleena. Even her rich red hair seemed to have lost its glow. It wasn't even a year later when I ran across her obituary in the newspaper. I cried. Not Marleena! She had been such an able, lively, and wonderful girl. Her time was up, and like Lyle and Kalie, her fight was over and God took her home.

Jillian, Kristen, and Amanda, 1994.

28
Should I Get My Child a Service Dog?

It was around this time between elementary and middle school that we decided to get a service dog for Amanda. We thought a dog would be a wonderful idea. In learning about

THE HELPING HAND

Getting a service dog is an individual decision, as each situation is unique. Be realistic when pairing a service dog with a child.

the many tasks that a service dog can carry out, the first exciting one was that it could help Amanda with her mobility. The dog would be trained to walk next to Amanda while Amanda held on to a handle on

the dog's pack. This would enable Amanda to execute long distances, like shopping malls and school hallways, without tiring or depending on help from another person. Other service-dog skills such as opening and holding open doors, pushing hard-to-reach elevator buttons, picking up items Amanda drops, and fetching items she requests all seemed like wonderful ways to make Amanda more independent. It would be a helper to Amanda and give us some relief from her care. That's not exactly how it turned out.

The whole family got excited at the prospect of having a pet. Until this time, all our pets had been caged ones, like hamsters and fish. Now we were getting a big dog! After visiting the kennel where the service dogs were trained, we drove home with sad news. The dog would be Amanda's dog only. The dog had to bond with its master. The other family members were not allowed to interact or play with it. Amanda's siblings had mixed emotions about that. Jillian's simple thought was that it was "just not fair." Kristen did not mind as much because she thought Starr was stinky. Can you imagine getting a dog and only allowing one of your children to be friends with it? Dogs and kids just go together, and Kristen and Jillian were not going to be able to pet Starr, play fetch with her, or even talk to her. They were very sad and jealous. I didn't blame them. I suppose we could have tried getting another dog for the other two, but I'm sure it would have been confusing for Starr. Besides, we didn't want to deal with the care and responsibility of more than one dog. And we'd never had a cat, so that sort of pet wasn't considered either.

Service dogs come into your home partially trained, at about a year to a year and a half old. After the phone call to say that our dog Starr was ready to pick up, we had to drive three hours to the kennel to get her. It was like going to bring home a new baby.

Our baby was a yellow Labrador-golden retriever mix. Starr was a very energetic dog, as well as lovable and smart. Once or twice a week, a trainer from the service dog place came and worked with Amanda and Starr. Starr would listen to the

PASS IT ON

Search the Internet under "service dogs" to find one of the many organizations near you that train dogs.

147

trainer. And Starr would listen to me. I was rather like the "alpha female" in the house, as Starr picked up that I was the mom and the boss around home. Amanda was learning how to handle Starr when her trainer was at the house. But when the trainer was not with us, I was the trainer. I told Starr what to do when she didn't do something after being told by Amanda. Little Amanda had a squeaky, weak, little voice that was hardly commanding or threatening, and Starr needed someone to give her commands with authority. Amanda tried to sound bossy and sure, and sometimes Starr obeyed. Whereas a sharp little snap on a leash should serve as a correction for a dog, Amanda simply did not have the strength to give an authoritative yank.

After weeks and weeks of training, Starr passed her certification test and was allowed to go anywhere with Amanda—from schools, to stores, to airplanes. School didn't exactly work out with Starr. Service dogs must be left alone so that they respond only to their owner. Here we had a big, huggable dog under the care and command of little squeaky Amanda, and they were at a *school*! A school is filled with lots and lots of kids. And the kids all love dogs. The kids also have lunches and pocketfuls of snacks. You just try to tell a school full of kids not to feed or pet a dog. And then let's put Amanda and Starr in a classroom of other special-needs kids and explain to *them* not to pet or feed the dog.

Starr ended up being more of a struggle for Amanda at school than a help. The temptations of food and attention from other students overwhelmed Starr and kept her from obeying Amanda. Starr also had much more strength and energy than Amanda. No matter what we tried, Starr would pull Amanda much faster than Amanda wanted to go. Starr could easily get a breeze going as she pulled Amanda briskly along the school hallway while Amanda held on in fear of crashing into the lockers.

Amanda and Starr.

On the positive side, Starr was Amanda's constant buddy and companion. No matter where Amanda was parked in her wheelchair, as soon as Amanda wheeled to another location, Starr was right behind her to follow and lie down by Amanda in her next parking spot. We gave Amanda the job of always scooping out Starr's dog food after she got home from school. That, at least, was one very important connection that Starr had with Amanda. The arrival home of Amanda meant dinnertime. And whenever Amanda dropped something on the floor, Starr was always there to pick it up for her.

Perhaps Ted and I were unrealistic to think that a service dog might replace us, somehow, and allow Amanda more independence. I believe the bottom line was that Amanda did not have the desire or capabilities to be totally independent. But Starr offered her selfless devotion and companionship. Ted and I felt better about leaving Amanda at home alone, because with Starr around, she was not alone. And a big dog at Amanda's side gave a sense of safety and security.

In her later years, Starr lost her hearing and most of her vision. Except for eating and an occasional trip outside to take care of business, Starr spent her days lying around sleeping. Oftentimes while working at the table, Amanda would drop something, and Starr would be roused from sleep by the sound or, more likely, the vibrations of the dropped object. You could almost see Starr roll her eyes; you were sure she was thinking, *Do I really have to stand on all four paws and pick that up for you?* Although she was not much of a "help" to Amanda in her later years, she was still a breathing, living, warm body that was always at Amanda's side.

We knew the end was near as Starr's health waned in her last months of life. There were several episodes of labored breathing, with extreme panting and gasps, resulting in a trip to the vet. Several episodes of what appeared to be seizure activity occurred. One time Starr collapsed in the front hall after coming in from outdoors, and we thought we were losing her for sure. After a hurried visit to the vet office and some emergency injections, Starr rallied. As Starr's health continued to decline, Amanda worried more about whether Starr was going to die. Starr had been at Amanda's side for a good dozen years.

Finally, on a warm summer afternoon, Starr returned from her visit outside and collapsed in the front hall. She wasn't getting up again. With her breathing labored, I couldn't even get her to lift her head. Ted and I pulled Starr into Amanda's room and laid Amanda down on the floor, nose-to-nose with her dog. Starr's labored breathing continued, but was slowing down. I got out my nurse's stethoscope to listen to her slowing heart. We told Amanda to talk to Starr and scratch her head. Amanda told Starr she loved her and what a good dog she had been. For almost an hour, Starr let Amanda pet her as her old doggy body slowed down. The breaths finally stopped, and there were no more heartbeats. We all cried. Hard. Amanda was very sad for weeks. It was months before we got used to that big old dog being gone. Starr was almost fourteen years old when she died.

Faithful friend.

29
Making the Grade at School: Good-Bye, Friend

By the time Amanda got to middle school, we all realized that she was not going to be able to continue with and pass the classes in the normal curriculum. That's when we switched her report cards to simply "pass" or "fail" grades. Most of the time she was passing by the hairs of her chinny chin chin. But it was better to "pass" than to see Ds and Fs on a report card. All this time, my prayers continued where I would ask God for there to be something that Amanda could be good at, prayers that she would find her "niche" and excel at just one thing.

> THE HELPING HAND
>
> *Handicapped children will feel more a part of the family and community if they can attend the same school as their siblings. See if you can change the grading on report cards to pass/fail so that they don't have the stress of poor letter grades.*

Throughout the junior and senior high school years, my younger two daughters were quite involved in a local theater group. Amanda loved going to watch her sisters, both at rehearsals and performances. She actually had a part in one show, *Alice in Wonderland*, where she played one of the Queen of Hearts's cards. The theater group was wonderful, and they always included special-needs kids when they could. In the show *Barnum*, a young girl in a wheelchair named Mindy got to participate as a clown in the crowd scenes. Mindy had been a normal little girl until a car hit her. She was injured quite severely and became a quadriplegic. Mindy had a tracheotomy and needed a machine to help her breathe. Her wheelchair was electric, and Mindy moved it by means of a simple joystick. Mindy always had a caregiver, either her mom or an aide, near her to take care of her needs. Mindy was bright, alert, well-taken care of, and an overall happy little girl. In her colorful clown costume and makeup, Mindy was ecstatic to be part of a show. The obituaries brought me the shocking and sad news about a year or two after the show that Mindy had passed away.

Like Amanda's earlier friend Kalie, Mindy had been another special friend in Amanda's life. And although the friendships were fleeting, the loss felt huge to me as the sting of death teased close to home. It's as if we parents of special wheelchair kids are watching our backs as we hope to not be the next recipient of death's sting.

Mindy was the fourth special friend that Amanda had lost. I cannot begin to describe to you the sickening hollow ache I got in my stomach with the news of each passing friend. I swear it felt as though our dragon were watching, because as we weathered the nauseating sadness of a friend's death, the air felt as though it were

---

WHISPERS FROM GOD

Ecclesiastes 3:1–2a *There is a time for everything, and a season for every activity under the heavens: a time to be born and a time to die.*

pulsating like a heartbeat from the whoosh-whooshing of the dragon's wings. There was a crushing sadness as well for the parents who had lost their child. And as sadness gripped my heart for the family who lost their little one, a sinister sense of relief toyed with my feelings as I tried not to show too much happiness that my own child had escaped death's grip this time.

I do not know how long Amanda will live on this earth anymore than I know the time of my own death. It's all in God's hands. I have to wonder why He takes some people home when He does and saves others for a longer time. For now, faith and strength from above must see us through.

Laurel, Jillian, Amanda, and Kristen, 1995.

30
Please Listen to the Patient's Parents! Bad, Bad Shunt

There was one very frightening time when, if Ted and I had not spoken up, Amanda would not be with us still today. Although her first year was plagued with shunt surgeries almost every month, it seemed like she grew out of that problem after turning a year old, and shunt surgeries became fewer and far between. Perhaps every couple of years, Amanda would have a spell of headaches and just not acting herself, and we'd take her in to the neurosurgeon. The diagnosis was usually a plugged or slow-running shunt, and she'd have surgery, get her new plumbing parts, and we'd go home happy with a properly draining shunt.

One time, in her late teens, it wasn't a plugged shunt that caused problems, but an infected one. That's bad. We're talking about shunt parts that are literally going into the brain to help drain off fluid, and the shunt itself has been taken over by bacteria—an infection. An infection in your brain is not good.

Identifying the shunt problem, this time, was quite different than the other times. Amanda's shunt had been located at various places on her head, as its location was often changed by the surgeon. Through the years, it had been on the left side of her head behind her ear, the same place on the right side, and one time on the front part of her head above her forehead but hidden under her hair. At this time, her shunt was behind her right ear. You couldn't see the bump it caused under the skin because her hair was long and thick enough to conceal it. For a few weeks, Amanda had been complaining of her neck being wet. I would wipe her neck with my hand and maybe feel a drop of water and would brush it off as sweat. But Amanda persisted in her odd complaint until I finally took a closer look. Combing her hair aside with my fingers, I felt for the familiar bump that marked the location of her shunt. I took a curious look at what I initially thought was tightly stretched skin covering the shunt. It was almost pearly and very tight and shiny, like scarred skin can look. Looking closer, I gasped when I realized that it was the shiny silicone surface of the actual shunt pressing through. Amanda's skin had thinned and finally broken open, and her shunt was exposed. The "water" she had complained about on her neck was actually the cerebrospinal fluid leaking out. Oh, I knew that couldn't be good. After phoning the clinic at the hospital, I was told to bring her right down. I wasn't feeling too scared because I figured that all they'd have to do was a quick little surgery to tuck that thing back in and sew the skin securely back up.

The nurse at the clinic shook her head after looking at Amanda's shunt and said she'd get Amanda admitted to the hospital. I asked if the surgeon would sew things back up and have us home the next day. The nurse replied, "Oh no, you are going to be in the hospital awhile." What I didn't realize until that moment was that with Amanda's scalp open and leaking cerebrospinal fluid, her shunt had acted like a wick and had sucked in any and all germs that Amanda's hair and head might have been exposed to. This would not be a quick replacement of shunt parts. Because of the infection, the entire shunt and all its tubing had to be removed. Amanda was then put on very strong IV antibiotics, and her shunt would be some temporary tubing that drained straight from her head into an external container that had to be kept sterile.

The antibiotics worked quickly, and except for the challenge of moving around the hospital with IV tubing and all the external shunt parts, Amanda was feeling pretty well while she waited for the antibiotics to rid her body of infection. After five days of antibiotics, Amanda went back to surgery to have all new shunt parts installed.

After surgery, it was a relief for Amanda to have the freedom to move about without the external shunt parts sticking out of her head. She seemed to be feeling fairly well except for a bit of a headache that we all attributed to postsurgical discomfort from being cut and stitched. However, as the day went on and the nurses talked about getting Amanda discharged from the hospital, it was obvious to Ted and me that things were not right. Amanda could not keep her eyes open and continued to complain that her head hurt. She acted as if her head were big and heavy like a bowling ball, and she could barely hold it up. If someone was standing next to her, Amanda would lean on his or her leg and rest her head against the person's thigh and close her eyes.

Both Ted and I were getting quite anxious and kept calling the nurses into the room. Repeatedly, the nurses kept trying to give Amanda more pain medication, including Tylenol with codeine and morphine as well. The nurses simply assumed her pain was from having surgery and that the answer was pain medication. Ted and I, the dumb parents, started to get a little aggravated that they weren't listening to us.

> **THE HELPING HAND**
>
> *Parents and caregivers must always go with their gut feelings. Better to err on the side of caution than to have a catastrophe. Remember, you are the advocate.*

Amanda always bounced back after shunt surgery. She wasn't bouncing this time. Our gut feeling was that something was wrong and Amanda was spiraling downward very quickly.

Ted and I pleaded our case with every nurse that came in to Amanda's room. We would explain to them that she just wasn't herself and how she usually bounced back after shunt surgery. As Amanda sat in her wheelchair, eyes closed, with her head leaning against my hip as I stood next to her, we begged the nurse and resident doctor to take a real good look at Amanda. Amanda struggled to stay conscious. The nurses kept offering more pain meds since they were convinced that Amanda was simply in pain. Ted kept pacing back and forth in Amanda's hospital room as frustration set in. The nurses were ready to have us sign her release papers and take Amanda home. Inside my head, I was screaming, "No, no, no! Something is very wrong with Amanda!" Ted at last spoke up and insisted that the doctor come take a look at Amanda. The nurses must have gotten annoyed with our frantic pestering, as they finally paged the surgeon for us.

The surgeon eventually made it to Amanda's room, took one look at Amanda, and sent her straight to the operating room. The new shunt was not working right and was plugged. Amanda's head was filling up with fluid very quickly. No wonder her head hurt—it probably felt like it was going to explode! And the pressure was causing Amanda to quickly lose consciousness. I shudder to think that if Ted and I hadn't been there and the nurses "helped" Amanda by doping her up with very strong pain medications that would have lowered her level of consciousness even more, she would have lost consciousness, slipped into a coma, and died. So for all of the teachers, doctors, nurses, and other professionals who are reading this book, I ask you to please listen to the dumb parents.

31
Surviving as a Family When a Child Is Hospitalized: The Hospital Life

Through the child-rearing years, Ted and I simply did the best we could and the best we knew how. We had no other family in the area to help us—no grandmas or aunts or uncles to help take care of our precious children. When Amanda had to be in the hospital yet again, Ted willingly stepped up to the plate to do whatever needed to be done. Usually that meant looking after our other two daughters while getting in as much of his workday as he could. It was just the way it had to be. Ted couldn't take off work every time Amanda was in the hospital, but he could help get the girls off to school or a sitter's each morning and go to work for the day. I went to the hospital to take care of Amanda. If the hospitalization was longer than a few days, Ted would offer to spend the night at the hospital to give me a chance to come home, shower, spend time with Kristen and Jillian, and sleep in our own bed. None of us liked it; we just did what we had to do.

The monotony of the hospital environment can be suffocating. If Amanda wasn't well enough to sit up in her wheelchair to take a walk down the hall, then we were stuck in her room. You get tired of watching television. You get tired of reading magazines. You just get tired.

Any visitor created a welcome break from the monotony. A visit from the doctor can be exciting because they usually bear news of when you might be going home. Even a nurse who lingers and takes time from her busy day to simply have a friendly chat is a precious thing. Visits from friends and family are the best. Like a little splash of friendship and sunshine, visits from loved ones can suddenly warm up the otherwise-cold hospital room.

If you can't make a visit, phone calls are just as welcome. Whether you call on the hospital room phone or personal cell phone, the call initially says the caller cares and took the time to phone. The ensuing conversation helps us get our heads out of the stifling confines of the hospital room, if only for a short time.

THE HELPING HAND

A parent's priority is to be at the bedside with his or her hospitalized child while his or her torn heart aches to be at home with the other children. Friends and family can help by remembering to give attention to the lonely family members at home as well.

If a person chooses to visit, it isn't necessary to be the bearer of gifts. Your visit is the gift. For all the balloons, flowers, cards, and stuffed animals people brought, Amanda many times was too sick to really care. It also made for a lot of stuff to have to pack up and cart home. If Amanda was feeling better, it would have been great for people to call ahead to see if there was anything they could bring for Amanda to eat. But you have to call first. Many times, when

161

a person is sick in the hospital, he or she may be on a restricted diet or not eating at all. A happy meal has the opposite effect if gifted to a child who is not supposed to eat it. If Amanda could eat, she often ate more if someone brought in a favorite fast-food item, instead of having to eat the not-so-palatable hospital fare.

> **WHISPERS FROM GOD**
>
> 1 Thessalonians 3:12 *May the Lord make your love increase and overflow for each other and for everyone else.*

A hospital visitor benefited me as well. Especially when Amanda was younger, she would fret if I left the room for any period of time. If someone showed up to visit, it was easier to leave Amanda under his or her watch for fifteen minutes or so, so that I could make a stop at the restroom and get a cup of coffee or a snack from the cafeteria. I would never plan to leave for long, but could relax and not feel hurried if I knew someone else was sitting watch.

It goes without saying that when a child is hospitalized, it affects the whole family. Neither Kristen nor Jillian liked their routines altered. They had to make do without Mom and tolerate any surrogates' attempt to keep things normal at home. To make matters worse, they would get this glimpse of Amanda hanging in the hospital with Mom all to herself and collecting gifts and flowers as well. It's a wonder they didn't wish to become hospital patients so they could collect on the balloons and such. In fact, when I recently asked Kristen and Jillian about how they had felt as children when Amanda was hospitalized, they both admitted being jealous of all the stuff Amanda got. It would have been great if more people would have occasionally stopped by the house and given Kristen and Jill a little attention. A trip for some ice cream, a sympathetic visit with a token candy bar, or a couple of simple balloons for the two brave little girls at home would have given Kristen and Jillian a little "you are special too" shot in the arm.

Many people offer to make and deliver meals to families when a family member is hospitalized. This happened often to us. It was always a blessing. Especially if Ted were taking on child care duties, it was wonderful for him to have dinner delivered. He was busy enough juggling work and the kids, so not having to cook or purchase a costly takeout dinner was a huge gift. Or if Amanda and I had just returned home after a lengthy hospital stay, it was wonderful to enjoy some home cooking when we were all too tired to cook. People were always so generous, with leftovers aplenty for several days' eating.

To Jillian and Kristen, I am sorry for all the times I was gone with Amanda in the hospital. And to those friends who supported us during those stays with visits, snacks, or even dinner for the family at home, Ted and I say, "Thank you."

But in all situations, when the hospital stay was over, there was nothing so sweet as getting home again. It just felt so good to be back in familiar surroundings with the family intact again. Like warm, sweet syrup, our separated family was now together again, and the warmth of home enveloped us as we fused our divided family back to sweet wholeness.

The Greshel Family, 2004.

32
High School or Special Education?
Finding the Right Placement

It was 1998, and Amanda had made it to high school. I had never dreamed that she would make it this far in the fifteen years that had passed since Ted and I started our family. During her high school years, I was happy to just have somewhere for Amanda to go each day. This sounds awful, but I am sure that every parent of a handicapped child out there will agree with me, that some days we didn't really care if our child was learning anything at school. We were just happy that someone else was supervising him or her and we had a break from the constant care.

By this time, Amanda was not taking any typical high school classes of history, algebra, or science. She couldn't understand or keep up with the class load. At our high school, all students with deficits or special needs were herded together

PASS IT ON
To see what programs your local school system has available for special-needs kids, go to the district website and search under "Special Services."

in one special education classroom for all or part of the school day. Some students attended half days at other school programs or handled some of the regular classes. To this day, I actually don't know what those students did in the special class. Sadly, the teacher in charge of that classroom was also the wrestling coach, and I recall Amanda telling me how the class once spent a few days with the teacher in the gym, washing wrestling mats. I really did not like hearing that mat washing was part of the curriculum. However, this tenured teacher was also up there in years, as well as challenged by his own health issues involving diabetes and being overweight. Amanda had related the mat washing story to me without complaining about it. I am fairly sure Amanda sat in her wheelchair and watched. If the other students had been upset with the task, I am sure complaints would have come from their parents. Many days, Amanda came home from school and would relate to me how the teacher had fallen asleep, again, and how the kids just kept busy by socializing with each other. She wasn't complaining. I know that if Amanda's whole school day had been spent in this classroom situation, I would have done something to change it. This teacher was nice enough, though, and Amanda enjoyed her special group of friends.

It was an interesting collection of students in this class. Some had cerebral palsy, while others were mildly autistic or mentally challenged to various degrees. They kind of knew they were each different, and they all had a special bond of camaraderie. God bless them all. As for the class and the teacher, I simply didn't want to stir things up for an older teacher who was tenured. Besides, Amanda only spent a half-day of school there each day. The other half, she was bussed to Jo Brighton Skills Center.

Jo Brighton Skills Center is a school for all kinds of kids and young adults with special needs. The school is full of many wonderful teachers, professionals, and paraprofessionals. Students are taught skills to get them jobs in janitorial positions, retail store stocking jobs, simple office settings, and kitchen work. The school, in fact, has a wonderful bakery and catering department that provides services to the community. At Christmastime, the cookie orders keep the phone ringing off the hook. Occupational and physical therapists work there to help students perform tasks according to their own abilities.

A special table was made for Amanda so she could work in the kitchen at Jo Brighton. Because Amanda is so tiny and in a wheelchair, she could not reach the regular counters used by all the other students. Working at her custom table, Amanda was able to help cut vegetables for the vegetable and dip trays that were put together, as well as take her turn at rolling dough and cutting out cookies. In reality, Amanda would never be able to work at a commercial kitchen with food preparation. She needed her own, lower work surface, she needed supervision, and she was just plain too slow.

If Amanda has any gifts, however, they include her ability to talk to people and to follow the rules. During the busy Christmas season when the phone kept ringing with cookie orders, Amanda proved invaluable. Amanda was great on the phone with people and could easily write down a cookie order. One holiday season it got to the point that the school had to declare, "No more cookie orders" because they were simply swamped with orders. The adult instructors, however, always felt pressured when a phone order would come in, and they would crumble like one of their own cookies and give in to yet another order placer. They quickly learned that if they put Amanda on the phone, she would tell the caller, quite matter-of-factly, that no more cookie orders were being taken at this time, thank you very much! And Amanda could not be swayed, because by golly, that was the rule!

In our state, schooling is available for special-needs individuals up to the age of twenty-six. Amanda fulfilled her four years in high school, attending commencement in her cap and gown and receiving her certificate of attendance in lieu of a diploma. Following that, she became a full-time student at Jo Brighton for the next seven years.

Amanda at her high school commencement, where she received her certificate of attendance, 2002.

Each year Jo Brighton helped Amanda with new experiences. Oftentimes, students were taken to several local nursing homes or assisted living facilities, where they served as companions or helpers during social and craft times. Of course, Amanda excelled at this, being the social creature that she is. There was one nursing home in particular where a certain elderly lady always waited for Amanda's visit. Amanda really enjoyed having a special friend who anticipated their visits together. Each time Amanda would come home from school and excitedly tell me how she sat with her aged friend; she told me all the things they had talked about that day. In this busy world, with people always hurrying here and there, it is a rare gift for a golden-ager to have a buddy to sit and chat with. Since Amanda loved talking and never rushed to do anything, she made the perfect comfortable companion. Amanda really enjoyed the nursing home visits that included a good chat time with a friend, especially if it smelled good there. I found it amusing that she also rated the various old folks' homes she visited by how good or how bad they smelled.

Other jobsite experiences included tagging clothes at a dry cleaner, straightening merchandise at a store, and rolling silverware in cloth napkins at a hotel restaurant. None of these experiences really thrilled Amanda, as they required physical agility, which Amanda found both challenging and tiresome. But if you needed someone to sit and listen, Amanda was the one to do the job.

By far, the greatest job for Amanda was in the local hospital pharmacy. Amanda's job was to either unwrap some kind of breathing inhalers or to put together "newborn packs" of several pharmacy items used for each new baby born. Amanda performed this job quite satisfactorily, but the best part was that the people in the pharmacy loved Amanda. They took the time to talk to her, and found her to be a funny and social little thing! Amanda loved their offer of friendship. To this day, she still chats with several of these great people, and even meets them once or twice a year at a local eatery.

Amanda "graduated" from Jo Brighton School in May of the year that she turned twenty-six years old. She was done with school. Like most graduates, she put on the typical happy face and cheers of a student celebrating being done with classes. I think she quickly realized that it was also the end of being able to go somewhere every day where there were friends and plenty of teachers and adults to chat with.

When I look back over the years, I realize that Amanda took from school only what she wanted, needed, and could grasp. That's Amanda for you. With her life full of so many challenges, she chose to keep it simple and to take only what was necessary. I can recall so many evenings through the years where she and I agonized over homework at the kitchen table. I wanted desperately for the proverbial light to go on in her head and for her to suddenly suck in and consume new knowledge, like a dry sponge to water. As I watched my other two daughters grow and learn and blossom, Amanda remained unchanged. I yearned for her to grow and develop, like the peeling open of delicate flower petals. I wanted to watch her bloom like her sisters and to smell the sweet floral scent of growth and maturity. She did not become a math whiz, a history buff, a promising artist, or an expert in any subject. She could get around in her wheelchair and perform the basic functions of hand washing and toothbrushing. But her skill level remained the same, although new goals were always presented to her. Content as to who she was and with the abilities she did have, it was as if Amanda closed the learning gate and decided that enough was enough. She was like a pretty little pink rosebud that refused to open,

I don't know when I gave up hoping that her brain would suddenly be "normal" and learning would just start happening. It was like I had to surrender my hopes so that I wouldn't be constantly disappointed. So many teachers and therapists would write pages and pages of goals for Amanda and speak to me of how we were going to get Amanda to do and learn new things. I would smile and agree. Inside, I knew that it was Amanda who was setting the bar. School, for Amanda, ended up being mostly a social outlet and a place for her to go each day to relieve me. Over the years, Amanda learned what she needed, and did a fantastic job of honing her social skills.

33
More Amanda Quirks:
Why Does My Child Do That?

Everybody has his or her quirks, including special-needs people. I am sure that I could poll the parents of children with any level of developmental disability and they could tell me stories about their child. The accounts would vary from strange habits, food preferences, and behaviors, to strange medical occurrences and mystery illnesses. I am sure we could fill a book simply on all of these strange phenomena. I've already described to you how a "dead soldier" empty bottle brought anguished tears, Easter bunny sightings resulted in waves of terrifying puke, and a growth-stunted Amanda kept doctors clueless. Amanda has continued to stump us through the years as well.

It was just three years ago, when Amanda was twenty-six years old, that we attended a wedding together. The bride was a girl who had been a caregiver for Amanda and had spent several nights here at the house. Amanda loved this girl and had been excited for weeks as she looked forward to the wedding and all the partying and dancing she planned to do.

The bride and groom happened to be big Detroit Tigers fans, and right after dinner when the music started playing, the mascot for the Tigers, Paws, showed up. Amanda went pale and started sweating. All her plans for the evening of dancing the night away suddenly evaporated with the simple desire to escape as fast as she could. Ted and I quickly pushed her wheelchair through the crowded room as fast as we could, trying to get her out before the puke of fear started. Ted and I were sort of glad, because we really didn't want to party late. Amanda was silent and shaking on the drive home but was able to hold the puke back and not lose her catered supper. Even Amanda cannot explain her fear. We teased Amanda a little bit for letting a costumed mascot cut her anticipated night of fun short. She was relieved to have gotten away from that scary guy, but quite embarrassed as well. To this day, her fear continues, as its origins remain a mystery.

Another mystery attached to Amanda has to do with her puking. As an infant, streams of projectile vomit could herald a bad shunt. Through the years, a sensitive gag reflex often reacted to textured foods and simple choking by an expression of vomit. Those puking occurrences we could explain. Besides the Easter bunny sighting regurgitations, in recent years Amanda has had many evenings of throwing up that we can't explain.

Amanda may have had a perfectly normal day of school and evening family time, but trouble would begin after bedtime. About an hour or so after we tucked Amanda in for the night, she would get herself out of bed. Frantically, she would roll into the kitchen in her wheelchair, looking for a puke bowl. The wave of nausea would hit, and Amanda would loudly puke herself inside out. Afterward, she would be drenched in sweat and require a complete change of clothes. At least two more waves of retching would follow, as Amanda would gag and choke up every last bit of stomach phlegm. After an hour or more of vomiting, clothes changes, and blow-drying sweat-drenched hair, the wave would pass, and we could finally tuck Amanda back into bed. The next morning, other than being tired, Amanda would appear to be just fine. She might even go to school and be completely normal all day. The next night, it might happen again, or it might not. Ted and I have had many an exhausting day after these late-night episodes. They sucked every drop of contents out of Amanda's stomach, and sucked a good portion of rest and calm out of Ted and me. It usually continued for one to three nights in a row, and then it would stop for months at time. We've never been able to medically explain why it happened.

Another strange quirk I observe in Amanda might be given the title of obsessive compulsive disease if I ever had her evaluated by a psychiatrist. I believe that because Amanda has so little control over her life, that she compensates by controlling as much as she can of her environment. She is absolutely anal about certain things in her room and her routine. Things in her room such as the box of Kleenex, picture frames, her alarm clock, and her desktop calendar have specific places where they sit; if you move them, she is crazy about putting them back in place.

Her bedtime routine is sacred, as she washes her hands and face and then brushes her teeth all in a particular order. We have two cordless phones in

THE HELPING HAND

The friend or family member you know who is a caregiver probably does not often get a good night's sleep. You don't need to remind us that we look tired. Instead, a little understanding goes a long way.

the house, and she is sure to put phone one on the phone one base and phone two on the phone two base. Don't you dare mix them up! Drawers have to be closed tight, towels hung straight, and everything must be in its place.

This compulsion has become quite an issue lately at bedtime. After putting Amanda to bed and closing her bedroom door, I will be called back to her room to straighten her covers or reposition the tubing from her Bi-PAP mask. She has been reprimanded several times for this behavior. Since she needs help literally getting into bed, I cannot go to sleep until I put Amanda to bed. Amanda is almost always up until eleven in the evening, so I, too, must wait until then to go to bed. After tucking her in, I usually watch about fifteen more minutes of television as I wait to make sure she is asleep and does not need anything else.

Amanda's bedroom is on the other side of the house from Ted's and mine. Once upon a time, Ted thought it would be a clever idea to put a bell on the table next to Amanda's bed. It's the kind of bell you see at a service desk, where you press down on the button on the top and it makes the bell ring. If you're like me, at the stores that have them, you never really want to smack hard on that button because it can emit quite a loud, harsh "ding!" That's the kind of bell Ted got Amanda, and it sits on the table next to her bed.

Here's the scenario: I have tucked Amanda into bed at 11:00 p.m. While watching mindless television, I struggle to stay awake on the couch as I wait to be sure Amanda is comfortably in bed and asleep. At 11:20 p.m., the silence of the past twenty minutes says I can finally tuck myself in bed. As I grab the remote to turn off the television, with

THE HELPING HAND

Do not buy a service desk bell. It will drive you crazy.

175

anticipation of my comfy bed and the ensuing sleep I crave so badly, I suddenly am stung by the sound of an obnoxious "ding!" I am so tired. Now I am so tired and angry. Stomping down the hall, I turn the handle to her bedroom door and swing the door open to ask her what it is she needs. Usually, she will ask if I can adjust her wheelchair sitting next to her bed into a better position or arrange the tubing to her Bi-PAP mask in a different way. My patience is gone, and I start to cry. I practically plead with Amanda to tell me just exactly what it is she wants so that I can go to bed. Realizing I am upset, she quickly decides things are arranged comfortably enough, and I leave her room, closing the door behind me. It is then another fifteen minutes that I wait, just to be sure things are really settled, before I finally get my chance to go to bed.

Like Popeye always claimed, I can hear the same declaration radiating from Amanda, "I yam what I yam." While many people may find her quirks endearing, they are constant reminders to me of Amanda's differentness—her deficits and deviation from normal. It is a waste of time and energy for me to criticize her, and for the most part, I can only whisper a prayer for patience when her actions start annoying me. When I try to look at life from her perspective and reflect on what Amanda can do, I am amazed at how long she has survived and thrived with the less-than-full deck she was dealt. When I think of how she has tolerated so many surgeries, listened to the disappointment of unfulfilled expectations from others, put up with stares from strangers, attempted challenges and tasks she could never complete, and endured a mother who has struggled to love and help her through the years, I am dissolved into a humbled, crying heap.

34

When the Caregiving Relationship Becomes Suffocating: Ways That Amanda Clings

I have recently become very much aware of how much Amanda uses me to get by each day. I don't mean in just the physical way, either. It's obvious that she is dependent on me for dressing, toileting, and lifting and transporting her places. But I have come to feel like I am a pseudo spouse to her. If she is telling someone a story and I am close by, she will almost always draw me in by saying, "Right, Mom?" There are even times when she may be struggling with the details of a story she is telling, and she will shrug and say, "Mom, you tell the story." So many times, it is

> ### THE HELPING HAND
>
> *Caregivers need to be sure to take time away from whom they take care of so that both of you can maintain some individuality.*

an old story that has been told already a thousand times, or it is really not very much of a story, and Amanda will draw me into the conversation by asking me to retell the story once again. I used to always respond as requested and tell the story for her. Lately, however, I have come to realize how strong her attachment is to me. I don't like it. It's almost a feeling of being her Siamese twin, her other half. In an attempt to keep myself separated from her, I will tell Amanda that I don't feel like telling her story and will encourage her to remember it and tell it herself.

There is also Amanda's frequent use of "we." She will ask what we are doing tomorrow, what we are eating for dinner, or where we are going. It's as though with everywhere Amanda goes and everything she does, Amanda brings me along. She needs me to pick up the slack and take care of the parts that she can't. Perhaps, with me she is whole. I can help make the tough decisions, finish the stories where the details have escaped her, know the plans for the next day, anticipate the needs that may come up, and untangle and straighten out other complexities of life. I can understand her dependency. But I also feel sucked into her existence to such an extent that I feel tethered to her and almost unable to think or plan without her being a factor. Who am I anyway?

Amanda is a great listener. When people are talking, she has all kinds of responses that reflect her interest in the conversation and fuel things to keep the discussion going. "Really?" "Nice!" "Cool, cool, cool!" "What?" "No way!" It's almost as if she is cheering them on and knows just how to keep the person talking. Once she gets hold of the end of that ball of yarn, so to speak, she grabs on real tight and starts to pull as the person unravels the story. If a joke is told, you can be sure Amanda will laugh wholeheartedly. Many times, after she has laughed quite dramatically at a story or joke told by whoever is in her company, I have asked Amanda if she understood the joke. Many times she's told me no, and

I've asked her why, then, did she laugh. Amanda has never really answered that question except to give a shrug that says, "Why not?"

Another way Amanda holds onto her audience is by literally holding on. She has learned that if she puts out her hand, people will automatically grab it as if to shake hands, and then Amanda just holds on. People are generally much too polite to pull away from her and will hold on until she lets go. I feel bad for some of her captives because you can see how uncomfortable they are with being "stuck" to Amanda. I have had to speak to Amanda many times about this. I have told her that she may have snagged and caught herself an audience, but that they learn fast and will not "take the bait" next time and will, in fact, even avoid Amanda for fear of being caught. I don't think Amanda agrees with me on this point. When I remind her that she has, once again, held on too long, she simply releases her hold and remains quiet. Sort of in one ear and out the other.

So how can a caregiver find independence and emancipation from his or her needy one? The simple solution is to take time away from the one you take care of. The difficult part of that solution is finding and making the time away. But some time away is better than none, and even small bursts of freedom can be refreshing. A trip to the grocery store can be quite an escapade when I take Amanda along. I have the added burden of loading kid and wheelchair in and out of the van, keeping track of the grocery cart and a wheelchair, and tending to Amanda's requests at the store while neglecting my shopping list. Although not the most exciting trip out of the house, the grocery store trip is a whole other venture when I go by myself. I can turn my interest toward the chatty magazines or linger in the cosmetic aisle and am far less stressed with only my cart and shopping list to tend to.

Another way to find release is to literally leave the house. Since Amanda could be by herself in our home, I had the luxury of going for a walk many times. I even trained to run a 5K one spring, and that actually was like my therapy as I put on my running shoes and left the stuffy house for the freedom of the open neighborhood streets. Early morning hours or late-at-night ones, when Amanda is in her bed sleeping, can also be therapeutic. Those are the times I can read a book or magazine, paint my nails, enjoy a cup of coffee, absorb a Bible study, or simply sit and think and pray. Maintaining my own identity so that I did not get sucked into living for her purpose only was key to facing the daily responsibility of taking care of Amanda.

35
Amanda's Tolerance for Me and Her Desire for Independence

I find it amazing that Amanda has been able to tolerate me for so many years. Like any normal adult, Amanda would probably love to get away from her parents and live on her own, making her own decisions and doing what she wants to do. Of course, Amanda is not "normal," and it has not worked out yet for Amanda to live independently. Therefore, she has to depend primarily on me for all her care. We are together a lot. We are together too much. And because I am her mom, I cannot help but give her constant advice, correction, and just a good healthy piece of my mind!

> **WHISPERS FROM GOD**
>
> Matthew 5:9 *Blessed are the peacemakers, for they will be called children of God.*

I don't like nagging her, but it just happens. On days when I feel like she has accomplished nothing and I've done everything (or so it seems that way to me), I know I get rather mean. Part of it is just my fatigue and frustration. It just bubbles out, and I spout off at Amanda. I believe Amanda knows that my bark is worse than my bite and that I just verbally unload on her sometimes. She has learned to just let me blabber. She lets my words go in one ear and out the other without taking it all personally. Amanda knows that within the next hour or later in the day, I will be calmed down and back to normal. She presents no argument or upset responses. It is quite like she tunes me out and lets me boil over.

_____

THE HELPING HAND
_____

A caregiver must find ways to release his or her anger and frustration before mistakenly taking it out on the one he or she is caring for.

Now if we are having a really bad day about something, I will do more than lecture in my half-crazy mom voice. The tears will come, and I will get close to hysterical with frustration. That's when Amanda listens and realizes that Mom is not just boiling over, she's exploding! Amanda has two responses to this scenario. I may have upset her so much that she, too, starts crying. When I see her upset and crying like that, it quickly brings me back to reality as I see this poor little broken girl doing the best she can and here I am screaming at her with unrealistic expectations. I feel awful. It's at this time that I usually leave the room and go someplace where I can cry even harder, but not where it will affect anyone else. Most times, I will apologize later to Amanda for getting so mad.

The other response is Amanda will fight back and yell at me. She will get angry and tell me how she is moving out and getting away from me for good. She is just plain sick of me and will yell at me that she is leaving. Like a small child, she has many times yelled, "I'm running away from home!" When she gets mad at me in response to my anger and wants to run away, it usually ends up with me laughing. Oh, how

I wish she really could run away to live on her own! I know that's not possible, so it's just so insanely funny to me. "Yeah, right, Amanda, you just go now!"

It wasn't more than a couple of years ago on a pleasant summer day that she got ticked at me and she decided she was running away from home that very instant. I was busy talking to the neighbor or something, and the next thing I know I see her in her wheelchair halfway down the street. She was making a break for it as fast as she could! I slowly walked down the street and easily caught up with her. I asked her where she was going, and she said she was off to live on her own. She wasn't sure where she was going, but there were a few friends she was thinking of that perhaps she could make their house by nightfall. I asked her if she had taken her cell phone with her. "No," she replied. I explained that if she were serious about running away, she should have packed a few things. Her phone might have helped her to reach a friend so she could check on arrangements for the night. She forgot to grab her purse, with her ID inside and money as well. She wasn't very happy when I turned her wheelchair around and pushed her home. I told her that, next time, she could run away all right, but perhaps she should plan a little better and grab a few things before making her escape.

Amanda has never unleashed any pent-up frustrations on me, mostly because she doesn't tend to hold on to anger. She may exhibit immediate angry annoyance when she is stumped with some physical task that challenges her. Or if Ted and I don't plan to go somewhere that she was hoping to go, Amanda might turn and wheel herself irately into her room. But once the irritation has diminished, and almost always by the next day, Amanda is back to being complacent and content. I suppose that, for Amanda, life is more about living for the day and making sure immediate needs are taken care of. To hold on to thoughts of anger or disappointment, with ensuing plans of change, are not part of Amanda's thinking.

She thrives on controlling her life by doing everything the same, day after day, comfortable with the familiarity of routine. The only downfall that creates is, as the years wear on, she is getting bored. With Ted and I slowing down a bit and enjoying our own activities in our semiempty nest, we have come to realize that Amanda really needs to be living somewhere that offers friends and activities in a group living situation. As we start considering moving Amanda out, excitement swirls as we think about how beneficial and fun it could be for Amanda. It is also terrifying.

As we begin toying with the idea of moving her out, we have looked at several living options and can't imagine making Amanda live in any one of them. And as Amanda mirrors our enthusiasm at how wonderful a new home would be for her, the enthusiasm quickly dissolves as the reality of moving out comes closer to being real. I would not make a good momma bird. It's starting to feel like I need to push this little bird Amanda out of the nest, and I just can't do it yet. Or I don't think Amanda can handle it yet. Seems like we are both fighting for control.

36
Playing the Part of Hospital Caregiver: Attention to Other Family Members

For every hospitalization, Ted and I had to plan our schedules around who was staying with Amanda and who was going

THE HELPING HAND

Whether you are caregiver to a needy child or adult, someone needs to accompany him or her during hospital stays.

to juggle the other girls at home. Except for when she was a newborn, either Ted or I would stay with Amanda during her hospital stays. Obviously, as a toddler, she was frightened to be in the hospital and was not the best communicator.

We needed to be there for Amanda's own safety.

As she got older, her communication skills got better, but her physical limitations made it scary for her to be alone in the hospital. She could not get from her hospital bed into her wheelchair, so if she were in the bed, she was stuck. She could not reach or move things on the bedside table or the bed table unless it was parked right in front of her. She needed assistance with reaching everything from the phone to a tissue for her nose. Even when she was an adult, we stayed with her, despite criticism from some people. "She's an adult," people would say, and couldn't understand why we had to be with her around the clock. Amanda sleeps on her stomach and, once placed in that position, pretty much stays in that position until morning. She can't roll over. Imagine this poor little girl lying in bed on her stomach with an IV attached somewhere, as well as other possible monitoring equipment. She's alone, and it's night. A nurse wakes her in the middle of the night to take her temperature and blood pressure, and then leaves the room. Amanda is now awake but can't reach the phone, turn on the television, or even sit herself up.

Besides the physical limitations, Amanda also has some mental limitations that made it necessary for us, her parents and advocates, to be there. Some tech person might come in the room to take blood for a blood test or want to take Amanda for an X-ray, and Amanda might not question whether it was a necessary test. Too much could happen or not happen without our knowing it if Amanda were left on her own. Besides, I think most any mother would want to be with her child during a hospital stay. Amanda's physical and mental limitations simply made it necessary for us to be there for her own safety. I've already related to you how Ted and I are sure she'd be dead already if we hadn't been with her during one hospitalization. Besides, it's just the comfort of having someone there that moves us to be with her. I would do it for any of my daughters, and I ended up doing just that.

During her sophomore year in college, our daughter Jillian ended up having gallstones that required surgery for her to have her gall bladder removed. We had to schedule the surgery during a long winter break weekend from classes. Ted stayed home with Amanda, and I went and spent two nights with Jillian; she was on the other side of the state in school. It was easier to find a surgeon over near the college and have her surgery there so that she didn't have to travel home to the other side of the state. I went the night before her surgery and took Jillian to the hospital early the next morning. I waited for her during surgery and was there postop. She was able to come home the same day as her surgery, and I spent the night with her and made sure she had everything she needed the next day before driving home. I would have stayed longer if I could have. And I would have dropped everything in the world to be with her during that time. She, too, was my baby! She was my own, and nothing was going to keep me from being there when she needed my help.

I also spent time with Kristen during her hospitalization. Kristen had been working at a summer camp when she suddenly fell and had a grand mal seizure. She was taken to the little local hospital, and when she had another seizure in the emergency room, was transferred to a larger medical facility in Grand Rapids. This all happened in the evening, and when I got the call that she had a second seizure and was being taken by ambulance to a bigger hospital, I left at ten o'clock that night and drove three hours to be with her at the hospital. Nothing was going to keep me from being with any of my daughters when they needed me.

Of course, this is a difficult concept for a small child to understand. I hope someday Kristen and Jillian will understand how difficult it was for me, as their mom, to leave them to be with Amanda during her hospitalizations. Even

WHISPERS FROM GOD

Matthew 25:36 *"... I was sick and you looked after me ..."*

187

though it was where I wanted to be, I hated every trip to the hospital with Amanda. Every trip to the hospital was a reminder of how broken Amanda's physical body was. For those of you who have experienced it, you know how being a "hospital mom" can be exhausting. You sit and worry, and worry and sit. The long hours tick slowly by as you wait for a visitor to break up the monotony or hope for a doctor with some encouraging news.

I would sit in the hospital with an aching burn in my chest, as I would long for home and family. If I could have cloned myself, I would have. The tug-of-war between the feelings of responsibility toward Amanda's needs and crushing guilt at abandoning my other two daughters just added flame to the burn. I hated it. I knew the two at home hated it. Little children simply want their mom to be there. Ted was doing all he could at home, but I'm sure those little minds were wondering why Amanda got all the attention.

Many times through the years, I found myself reminding the people around me that I have other children besides Amanda. There's this big label on my forehead that reads "Amanda's mom," and I get angry that my other children aren't acknowledged and that a daughter in a wheelchair portrays my identity. I suppose it is natural for most people who know me to always ask about how Amanda is doing, because there have been so many scary, sick times for her over the years. It is nice that they ask.

But there are all kinds of acquaintances from church choir rehearsal and Amanda's former school, to people I regularly see while out with Amanda at stores and doctors' appointments, who think I am only Amanda's mom. I will often pipe up in a casual conversation something about one of my other daughters. "My daughter Kristen did this" or

"My daughter Jillian went there" or "I went to visit my daughter Kristen" or "My daughter Jillian used to do that." I am quick to include and brag about my other two. It is not untypical for people to respond, "Oh, you have other children?" Why wouldn't I have other children?

It's almost as if Amanda and I are literally bound together as one person. So perhaps part of the reason I am always recognizing my other children publicly is so I can try to stand as a separate person. Once again, it is because of that stifling, suffocating feeling of being so closely entwined in Amanda's physical, daily life that I have to publicly and regularly peel her attachment off of me. Who am I anyway?

37
Thinking about Her Dying

Normal parents of normal children don't usually think or talk about their child dying. When parents have a baby, they tend to think and plan for that child's lifetime, which they assume will last sixty, seventy, eighty, or more years. With a child who has a sickness or disability, a parent will ponder the child's death from time to time. We really do. You may think this is awful, but I know enough parents of special-needs kids and it really is thought about.

Because Amanda has been hospitalized several times with situations that were potentially near death, we have felt death's call. We know death lurks close for our child, and it is a reality that we have faced and may face sooner than others. Occasionally, I wish that I could know when Amanda's last day will be. It really would help in making some decisions. Now that she is twenty-nine years old, I am tired of taking care of her

WHISPERS FROM GOD

Ecclesiastes 8:7–8a *Since no one knows the future, who can tell someone else what is to come? As no one has power over the wind to contain it, so no one has power over the time of their death.*

and would love to have her moved to a home of her own. But what if we only have one more year with her? What if we have less than a year? I certainly wouldn't move her out if I knew time with her were short. But, if she is going to be around for five, ten, or more years, then maybe she should move to a place where she can enjoy her life with other housemates and activities. It sure would help to know. But I am scared that I might find out that she will be leaving us soon. I also am scared that I would find out that she is going to be around a very long time. Either extreme has its fears for me. I am scared she could die tomorrow. I am scared she'll never leave me and forever be my responsibility. I decide each time that it's better not to know.

When I think of Amanda dying, I also think about how it will happen. Will her kidneys wear out, and will kidney failure make for a long, slow death? Will she get an infection that goes systemic and wreaks havoc on her little body before we can fight it off in time with the correct antibiotic? Will the shunt in her head fail without our noticing and result in her brain function stopping when her head succumbs to too much pressure? I really do think about it, because she has so many more health threats than a normal person does. Naturally, the more health issues a person deals with, the more likely it is for sickness to happen. I hope Amanda does not have to endure a sickness that would take her slowly away from us. She hates hospitals and has, obviously, had more than her share of hospitals, tests, and multiple procedures. It wouldn't be fair for her to die in the cold, unfriendly hospital while possibly in pain, fear, and sadness. If Amanda were sick and dying, I wouldn't be able to stand to see her so sick and scared. I wouldn't want that for her.

Strange that I am almost wishing I could choose how she would die. Sometimes, after she's been sick with much puking and sweating spells, I will finally see her sleeping comfortably and I almost wish that God would come scoop her up to heaven. If and when she dies, I think Amanda deserves a peaceful end without any long-suffering or pain. God could just rock her to sleep and carry her home. I both cry and smile when I think of her in heaven, in her completely whole body, laughing and skipping on those golden streets. No more struggles, pains, discomfort, frustrations, or challenges.

Amanda is an early riser. Her average wake-up time is probably six in the morning. I wish she would sleep in. It is funny how, when she sleeps in like I wish she would, it also stirs a panic in me. *What's wrong?* I start thinking. *Is she sick? Oh, dear Lord, she didn't die in her sleep, did she?* Then I tiptoe near her room to try to hear her breathing, careful not to get too close to her door and wake her with the sound of the creaking floorboards. My heart beats faster as I nervously go about getting myself a cup of morning coffee, while keeping my ears attuned for the sound of her getting out of bed. After what seems like an eternity of waiting, I finally hear the "click" of her seat belt, followed by her rolling into the room. Another night and God let her stay here.

Amanda sitting on our boat, 2001.

38
Finding Doctors and
Professionals Who Care

Many times through the years, the challenges of taking care of Amanda have extended to the services that are supposed to be helping her. Over the years, there have been times of no help, or helplessness dealing with doctors and medical services. When Amanda was young, we always saw a whole team of doctors at Children's Hospital. These doctors and professionals specialized in patients like Amanda and were compassionate and dedicated to helping. When Amanda got older, she no longer could see the Children's Hospital doctors, and she became a recipient of government Medicaid insurance and medical personnel.

THE HELPING HAND

Professionals should not assume a patient's motive, economic level, intelligence, or character. On all levels, respect should be reciprocal.

With her frequent urinary tract infections, I thought it best to seek out a urologist to handle her care. After searching the Medicaid website, I finally located a urologist that Amanda could see. My first appointment, I simply wanted to meet the doctor and establish a doctor-patient relationship. After long lines, a healthy dose of paperwork, and an hour-and-a-half wait, it was finally our turn. The doctor came into the room, sat down, and started writing. I introduced Amanda and myself and gave a brief history. I explained how we were looking for a doctor to follow her in her care and described her frequent urinary infections. The doctor never introduced himself and barely looked at us. He simply asked what it was we wanted that day. I was rather dumbfounded. In hindsight, perhaps he was used to writing prescriptions for patients to renew their meds and pain pills. I didn't know. He remained seated and did not even touch Amanda. Figuring he needed to do something legitimate, he scribbled off a prescription for a kidney ultrasound for Amanda and said he'd see us next time. I believe this particular urologist had a regular practice in a urology clinic and worked a few days a month for the Medicaid insurance program. He showed us no respect and, obviously, did not want to be there at the Medicaid clinic that day. I left in tears with Amanda and never went back. We still don't have a urologist.

Another time, we needed help with repairs for Amanda's wheelchair. Amanda sits on a fabric-covered gel pack that is squishy for her tushy and helps prevent bedsores or pressure sores on her hiney. The "squish" had squished out of her cushion, and the fabric was torn and threadbare. When calling medical places, you can get nothing without first revealing every bit of information about your medical insurance. I tried tracking down the people who made Amanda's current wheelchair, but they passed me on to someplace else. Everyone kept passing me on, either because they did not make the chair, so they did not want to make the repairs, or there was an insurance holdup. I finally prefaced all my phone calls with, "I need repairs for my daughter's wheelchair, and I'm willing to pay cash." That didn't work either! The repair places just didn't know how to process work without insurance info. It took me months to get those things fixed and replaced.

Finding good doctors and medical services is never an easy task. That's just the way it is. There are good ones out there; you just have to find them. If you have a bad experience with one, don't wallow in the bad care, but move on. Good ones do exist.

The easiest thing to do is simply ask around. I have often passed on my own recommendations when friends have inquired about what dentist I go to, what hair stylist does my hair, or what painter I've hired to paint a room. If you have networked with a special group, either through the Internet or by attending meetings, ask for advice.

I also advise patience when dealing with new doctors and medical services. Change always means completing piles of paperwork. That's also just the way it is. With new contacts, records have to be shared, signatures completed, and authorizations given. Most of the office people you will deal with get tired of all the necessary forms, too, but they are a required part of their job. One time, after trying to be the middleman in getting some information faxed from Amanda's doctor to a medical supplier, I could sense a little exasperation from the front desk ladies. I was sure I was being a pest with my phone calls in trying to get the right papers faxed. A few days later, as I had to take Amanda in for a doctor's appointment, I made a point of saying "Thank you" to the office ladies and added a bag of chocolates to my expression of gratefulness. The hardworking ladies were sweetened up by my acknowledging their efforts, and my label of being a pest was removed.

39
A Caregiver Needs Her
Own Identity: Coping

The opening song in the Broadway musical *A Chorus Line* includes the lyrics: "Who am I anyway? Am I my resume?" I sing that song a lot. I understand that what you do and who you surround yourself with defines who you are. I am around Ted all the time, so people identify me as Ted's wife. When the kids were in school, we saw other moms and kids, and we were always "Katie's mom" or "Ben's mom" or "Kristen's mom." But after over twenty-nine years of being "Amanda's mom," I think I may be having an identity crisis.

Having been born and raised in the same community, Amanda has become a familiar person in this area. Anyone who went to high school when Amanda was there will remember "that little blonde girl in the wheelchair." In fact, I think my two other daughters have found that to be true. They will run across old high school acquaintances and find that people usually remember Amanda, or that all you have to say is, "I was Amanda's sister ... you know ... remember that blonde girl in the wheelchair?" Yeah, so who am I anyway?

Invariably, when I am out shopping with Amanda, someone will come up to her and say, "Hi, Amanda, remember me?" Of course, I don't know who the heck they are, but they know Amanda. From elementary school to high school, from church and all the places that Amanda went to school, she is a familiar sight to many. A few years ago, we advertised my daughter Jillian's pet hedgehog for sale. I had a woman call who came over to consider the purchase of this funny pet. As soon as she walked in, guess what she said? She exclaimed, "Hi, Amanda, remember me?" It was a woman who had worked at Amanda's school many years earlier.

Although it was many years ago when she naively referred to me as Cinderella on the day I was scrubbing the plant pot dirt from the kitchen floor, that Cinderella feeling remains. With Amanda, I still feel like I am trapped in my dark little corner of the fireplace, with neither the time nor the resources to go to any ball. If it is a day in which I am supposed to go to work, I must first be sure to get Amanda fed, dressed, toileted, and her hair washed. It sounds so simple, but oh how I would savor the idea of getting up and getting ready for work with no one to think of but myself.

Now I understand that when you have kids, that's just part of the job: getting your small children ready for the day. But Amanda is twenty-nine years old. I have been doing this for twenty-nine years. Once I get her ready for the day and hurry myself along as well, the care continues. Fortunately, I work close enough to home that I can come home at lunch, but I am sure to make a lunch for Amanda in case she gets hungry before I get home or if work gets too busy for me to have more than a few minutes at lunchtime.

Then there's the issue of cathing. I must get home at lunch to cath Amanda, or else she will be sitting in a puddle of pee. If I can't make it home, I must arrange for someone else to stop by and cath her. When I finally do make it to work, I can expect several text messages and even some phone calls while I am trying to work. So, yes Laurel, you may go to work *if* you first wash, toilet, and dress Amanda, then feed her breakfast and lunch, and be sure to come home at lunch to take care of bathroom needs again.

The trials and tribulations of raising children can be daunting. If your child is handicapped, it only compounds the challenges. As a parent, strength, support, sympathy, ideas, relief, and camaraderie are drawn from friends and family. So many times I felt alone in facing the challenges of Amanda. During my times of anger and frustration with God at my circumstances, I would cry out, "Why did you leave me alone, God?" I felt sad when friends would gleefully tell me of overnight plans where their children were in the care of family. Or friends who took trips with their spouses—just the two of them—while the kids stayed with Grandma. Doesn't this mom of a handicapped child deserve that more than the others? I would berate God for giving Amanda to the wrong family. I needed a family with lots of support: a family with sisters and cousins and grandparents who were willing and able to lend a hand to help this tired mom.

> ### THE HELPING HAND
>
> *As a caregiver, accept whatever help you can get. Close friends and family may not offer the help you are looking for, but accept it and move on.*

On the list of questions I plan to ask God when I finally stand in line at the pearly gates is this: "Why didn't you give me a large family to help me?" I have cried many tears at the loneliness. I have fallen on my knees next to my bed in despair and asked God what I was doing wrong. Was I so bad and undeserving? The feelings of abandonment and loneliness would be crushing at times. I would cry so hard that my nose would plug up and I would feel like I was suffocating. The bubbling pot of emotions that I was would spill over with the hot tears that fell from my eyes. Breathing would turn to gasps. The pain of sadness and despair at this point was so intense that I would have to pinch myself very hard to actually cause a physical hurt to match the emotional pain. Then I would suck it up, put a lid on my emotions, blow my nose, and go back to life.

As I look back over the years, I try to identify how I was able to cope and find a sense of self. This is really a common challenge for all mothers, as the constant care of children overwhelms the days. Because my "child" is twenty-nine years old, with the addition of exceptional medical needs, I have been in caregiver overload. But the same rules of coping exist. However you can, you must find ways to get away and do things that you can only do alone. I've already mentioned my 5K training, where I could both do something Amanda couldn't do with me and it got me out of the house for about forty-five minutes each day. I believe part of my drive for going back to school to become a nurse was not only a literal way to get out of the house, but it challenged my mind and I had the sense of personal accomplishment of becoming an RN. I enjoy singing, so attending church choir practice on Thursday evenings serves as a short respite. Whether it's for a walk around the block, a twenty-minute quiet time with a good book, a stop at the bar with a friend for a drink, a weekly yoga class, a

WHISPERS FROM GOD

Even Jesus took time away from His caregiving.

Luke 5:16 *But Jesus often withdrew to lonely places and prayed.*

professional manicure, or a late-night soak in the tub, a caregiver must find ways to self-indulge and edify. A tired, worn-out, miserable caregiver is of no use to anyone.

40
Divorce in Families with Special-Needs Children

I am sometimes jealous of my divorced friends. I would give anything to only have Amanda every other week. Even having every other weekend free would be a luxury. Divorce, of course, can happen to any marriage. I have heard that the statistics are high for couples with handicapped kids. I can sure understand why.

Any typical mom has her days when she is just tired of feeding kids, doing laundry, wiping noses, trying to keep the house clean, as well as dealing with sibling rivalry, cuts and hurts on small bodies, and running kids to school and sports. With Amanda, I also had days that included doctor visits to the hospital in Detroit. There was extra time spent to help Amanda dress, wash, and complete all her bathroom needs as well. When Ted came home from work, there were many days I would simply want to run away! He was pretty good at taking over when I needed a break. Oh, but there were plenty of times when I wanted to leave!

I really can't fathom how marriages can survive without having faith in God. As a Christian, I find myself daily seeking God's will and hoping to be a good person, based on guidelines from the Bible. Jesus set the example of how to be truthful, loving, patient, slow to anger, and forgiving. It is with these qualities that I hope my husband treats me, as well as how I try to treat him. We also vowed before God and witnesses on our wedding day that we were uniting as one till death us do part. Without those guidelines or standards, there is no security, no structure, and

> PASS IT ON
>
> *There are different reports concerning divorce rates of parents who have children with disabilities, but most studies agree that there is a high level of marital discord in these families and that divorce or separation is more likely in families of children with more severe and impacting types of disabilities.*
>
> R. M. Hodapp and D. V. Krasner. *"Families of children with disabilities: Findings from a national sample of eighth-grade students."* Exceptionality 5 (1995): 71–81

no discipline to keep the marriage on any right course. In fact, the relationship would have no bars and no map of design or outcome. Fortunately, both Ted and I believe Jesus Christ to be our Savior and draw strength and direction from Him. And I believe most couples who wed in a church are at least acknowledging the presence of Christ in their lives as well. But we all experience situations in our lives when our faith is tested. Infidelity, job loss, major illnesses, and untamed tempers are all tests to a marriage that can test our faith as well.

I can tell you that through the years, there were many times that I felt like I was holding on to my faith in God by mere fingertips as I struggled with the challenges of being Amanda's mom. There were so many times I wanted to give up and get out. In agony, I would feel like I wanted to explode from the pressures of life. I am sure my blood pressure soared when I found myself in what I called my "sledgehammer mood." The "sledgehammer mood" was when I just wanted to swing a big hammer with every ounce of strength I had and destroy everything around me. I envisioned mirrors and glass shattering as I swung and allowed things to shatter and crumble. Thankfully, I never got to actually destroying anything; I never actually acted out as I felt I wanted to. Eventually, the pressure and stress subsided, and I would get a grip on reality. God's grip on me held strong as I battled another extreme day. Sadly, I can easily imagine how faithless, frustrated parents could allow the anger to take over, causing both emotional and physical harm to those around them. I believe that Satan has a great time in these situations, when spouses or parents lose control and let evil take over. Thank you, Jesus, for never letting go of me.

Divorce is so sad. Oh, I believe it is necessary in some situations. But through the years, Ted and I have had many friends whose marriages have ended, and we've shaken our heads in disbelief. So many times, we've seen a happy, healthy family suddenly break up. These are families where Dad has a great job, the house is lovely, the kids are all healthy and thriving, and there may even be a cottage up north, and loving friends and grandparents aplenty. But then, the mom or dad decides that they don't love each other anymore, or they love someone else, or they love something else. Perhaps they've grown bored with life or just want a change. Maybe they just need to spend more time together, but instead choose to spend no time.

When Ted and I have seen marriages like this fall apart, we simply weep at what we see. We want to literally shake these people and give them a slap on each of their cheeks. We would love to scream at them, "Don't you know how lucky you are?" Thank goodness I have a husband who loves me and is committed to us. Thank goodness for our faith in God. Despite the pain and challenges we've had over the years with some of life's usual barbs, but especially with Amanda, I can honestly say that God has blessed us richly. Perhaps it is the tough times that make the good times seem so sweet. It is the faith of knowing that, despite the bad times, God has a strong hold and will lead us through to someplace good. As the trials through the years serve to cement Ted and me together more solidly with trust and love, perhaps our divorced friends may someday look with jealousy at us.

41
Sick and Tired of Giving Care: Finding a New Home for Amanda

My time away from Amanda not only helps me with my own identity, it also serves to refresh and revive me. Whether it is a walk around the block or a long hot shower, time away is mandatory for any caregiver. If it can be arranged, a day or a weekend away is even better.

There were two summers when we were able to take Amanda to a camp for handicapped kids. After finding someone to take our other two daughters, Ted and I actually had the taste of almost five days without kids. Without having to cath Amanda, lift Amanda, help Amanda, dress Amanda, or consider Amanda in every minute of our day, I experienced complete liberation. I felt like Eve in the garden with her tempting apple, salivating for more of this forbidden fruit of freedom. It was such a release and a freedom to be without kids, particularly the never-ending demands of Amanda.

PASS IT ON

Search the Internet using the words "special-needs camps" to find numerous camps with various specialties.

Oh, it tasted delicious. I actually sighed in blissful satisfaction as I savored the fresh feeling of independence. It was so good a feeling it felt almost sinful. I was enjoying it way too much. I recall many times saying, "Oh, I could get used to this." So maybe God knew better than to let me get too many tastes, knowing that it wasn't really available to me.

Most of my breaks from motherhood and Amanda came in small doses. Every once in a while, Ted and I would get away for a night or two. We'd train a friend on how to cath Amanda, and I would spend hours writing notes and organizing things so that I would feel comfortable leaving Amanda in someone else's care. That appetite for a night of freedom was so intense, the resulting getaway was worth all the planning I had to do. It was always a great investment of time and money, because of all the preparations as well as the money I would pay the caregiver. An evening out was precious, too. How wonderful it was to go to dinner or a friend's house without the interruptions of little girls! Any normal couple can appreciate the adult time a night out offers.

With Amanda older now and the other two daughters out of the house, time away has become even trickier to arrange. Although Amanda can stay by herself, there are many reasons she is not left alone. First and foremost, I feel sorry for her. Since school has ended for Amanda, she is home a lot and does not have the luxury of numerous friends to come and go with. She hates being alone. She gets so lonely, my heart breaks for her, and I feel guilty leaving her.

Then there is the issue of who will get her meals for her and who will cath her. Leaving her for several hours takes planning. I must make sure her physical needs are met and that she possibly has someone coming over to spend some time with her.

I have a dear friend who daily took care of her mother, who was wheelchair-bound and needed much assistance. Her mom lived with her dad in their own home, but my friend went over every day to help her aging parents with cooking, cleaning, and whatever else needed doing. She struggled with feeling the fatigue of being a caregiver for so many long years. She said what helped her was to remind herself that she would rather be the caregiver than the one receiving the care. Her statement really made me think. It made me cry. Oh Lord, I would give anything for Amanda to not have her handicaps and to be grown up and thriving, walking and running and living a full, normal life. And when I try to imagine myself in her position, it is awful to think of how dependent she must be on people.

On the days when her requests for help with things start sounding like demands to me, I remind myself that I would not want to be in her position. Can you imagine not being able to quench your thirst with the drink in front of you? Amanda's hooked on diet Coke, and there have been thirsty times when she's gotten the big two-liter bottle of Coke out of the refrigerator and managed to get it over to the table. But if the last person pouring Coke happened to twist the cap on too tightly, Amanda's weak little hands will not be able to loosen it. She will try for a minute or two, and then she will either hope someone comes along to open and pour a drink for her, or she will give up and put the bottle back in the fridge. I try to help her out quickly and without complaining whenever she asks, as long as it's not something I know she can do on her own.

There are times when I can't stand to touch Amanda. I'm sure this sounds just awful to you. Perhaps overwhelmed parents of other special-needs children will relate. I get tired of doing so much for Amanda, including care that requires touch. There's cathing, dressing, and washing her hair, among all the constant daily assistance. When I help to pull on or off her slacks, I have to pick Amanda up, and she grabs hold around my neck and holds on while I either pull up or pull down. As she holds on, I feel like she is literally choking me, and I feel like I am suffocating. In reality, I can breathe just fine. It is just a feeling of her seeming like a constant sticky and persistent little person, rather like the little baby monkeys you see clinging to their parents. Perhaps it is a bit of claustrophobia that makes me feel that way. I just know that I almost cringe when she's clinging to me, and I just want to peel her off as if she were a hot, itchy, tacky piece of flypaper. It's a smothering feeling, and I just want to be let go so I can escape and breathe some fresh air. By the time I am done taking care of Amanda's needs, I don't want to touch her anymore. Literally.

And then when I think about it, I feel awful. Here's little Amanda in her wheelchair, who loves to hug people and never gets to sit on a couch to snuggle with anyone. Granted, it's partly by her own choice, because she prefers to stay in her

PASS IT ON

Fifty-one percent of care recipients live in their own home, 29 percent live with their family caregiver, 8 percent live in someone else's home, 4 percent live in nursing homes, another 4 percent live in assisted living, 3 percent live in independent living or retirement housing, and the last 1 percent report "other."

Caregiving in the United States; *National Alliance for Caregiving in collaboration with AARP, November 2009* wheelchair all day. But her lifestyle keeps her from playfully wrestling on the floor with a pet or even a friend, as well as ever simply cozying up to anyone. It helps me to understand and tolerate how she hugs everyone who is either coming or going. Oftentimes, however, she will hug and not let go for inappropriately long times. For most people, hugging Amanda means bending over, and I know from experience that bending over like that can really hurt the back in a short time. Many times, I have had to tap Amanda mid-hug of somebody and tell her to let go. I am thankful that so many people help to fulfill Amanda's needs for touch, and never hesitate to hug her when she sits there with beckoning open arms.

I am so tired of taking care of Amanda. But I am stuck. For most people in the situation of a job they don't like or a relationship that's bad, a not-so-good club they belong to, or even uncomfortable living circumstances, they can usually make changes to find their way out. They can look for a new job, end the relationship, quit the club, or move to a new address. I can't quit this job. Amanda is my daughter and my responsibility. Ted and I are currently trying to find a good home for her, apart from us, but that has quickly become a huge challenge. It's hard to let go, and it's hard to find a good place where we can entrust the care of our daughter to someone else. Our main priorities are that she will be happy where she goes to live and that she is well taken care of. We have come close too many times to losing her to illness, so it is hard to let go and trust that someone else will know when she is dangerously ill.

We are still looking, and praying that God has a plan for her. I am at the point where some days I find myself screaming (to myself, of course), "I hate you, Amanda, I hate you." I know that sounds awful. Some of you will understand, though. I have actually told people that Amanda and I have a love-hate relationship. Of course, we love each other, but we hate the dependency Amanda has. I have realized that we really have to find a place for Amanda because I am getting to the point where I am very angry and losing my identity. There is a lot of resentment inside of me for having to take care of her so much. And I don't blame Amanda; it's just the way it is. If I could find my way back to being "me" and we could live our own separate lives, perhaps I could even find that I can enjoy Amanda more with occasional visits instead of the constant 24/7.

So what are Amanda's options? If money were no object, we could simply move her to a house or apartment and hire staff to take care of everything. Due to lack of finances, that's not going to happen. Moving along to the next option, there are "group homes" that take in developmentally disabled adults. From what I've come to find out in my searching, these can be quite difficult to find and even harder to find the right "fit" for Amanda. Some homes take in adults who have extreme physical needs. These adults have very little, if any, communication skills and are wheelchair-dependent, without the ability to move themselves at all. Workers in the homes must dress, feed, wash, toilet, and give complete dependent care to these adults. Although Amanda

> PASS IT ON
>
> *Fourteen percent of family caregivers care for a special-needs child, with an estimated 16.8 million caring for special-needs children under eighteen years old. Fifty-five percent of these caregivers are caring for their own children.*
>
> Caregiving in the United States; *National Alliance for Caregiving in collaboration with AARP, November 2009*

has many physical needs, she can do quite a bit herself, is able to communicate, and enjoys social settings. She would be bored from lack of social interaction in this kind of home. There are also homes and communities that consist of Down's syndrome adults. These adults usually can take care of most of their physical needs and are able to interact with each other and work at simple jobs. Amanda would not fit in there because of her wheelchair and all the physical help she needs. It really is a daunting task for parents of disabled adult children. It is so difficult to find a good fit for our children. We want them to be happy. We want them to be safe.

For any caregiver who shares my burden of thinking we are the best at what we do, we are destined to our lot in life, or we should not surrender our duties to anyone else, I beg you to listen. Unless we take time for ourselves, pursue other interests, talk about other subjects besides whom we take care of, or simply learn to think independently, we risk becoming martyrs. And no one likes a martyr. So skip the "poor me" routine and take time for yourself however you can.

My time away from Amanda is precious and little. But any break I get, large or small, is welcome and treasured. Whether it is a couple hours shopping at the mall, an evening out with friends, or a weekend away, the time spent separate from Amanda helps me keep a little bit of my own identity. I get a chance to be more than just "Amanda's mom." If you happen to be reading this book because you know someone with a handicapped child, please give that "someone" an hour or more if you can.

42

Family Situations Are All Unique:
Do We Move Her Out or Not?

I have seen several families who have kept their special-needs child, now adult, at home with them. God bless those caregivers! I must keep in mind that each family situation is unique, with factors such as finances, family support, and the extent of handicap affecting each.

At the office where I used to work, there were two families that I often think about. Again, names will be changed for privacy purposes. There was one couple who had two children. One child, a daughter, was grown, with children of her own. The other child, a son, was still living at home with them and was older than my Amanda. Their son, Dennis, had Down's syndrome. Dennis could walk, talk, feed himself, dress himself, and use the bathroom. He actually was quite able, just needing direction due to his lack of good judgment and reasoning. He was like a little boy and was really only lacking mentally, not physically like my Amanda. I believe they took Dennis everywhere they went, but had other family members who would take Dennis from time to time when his mom and dad wanted some time alone. I recall one day when Dennis's dad spoke to me about how wonderful Dennis was and what a special blessing he was. He did not know that I had a special-needs daughter. I felt guilty listening to him about how special he thought his son was. I was not sharing similar thoughts about my own child. Oh, yes, I think Amanda is special, but I was not feeling so joyful about her being my constant tagalong companion. Dennis and his parents went everywhere together. But I know that these parents also could easily leave Dennis with someone and go on a vacation for a week. They didn't have to worry about lifting and moving a wheelchair or all the physical needs that my daughter requires. For this family, their special-needs child lived at home and everyone was happy.

There was another family who came to the office that grabbed my attention. There were just the two of them. Mom must have been in her seventies, and always had her daughter, Betty, with her. I am guessing that Betty was somewhere in her fifties. Betty had been a normal, healthy baby until the day, as a young child, when she was hit by a car. Brain damage left her with the mentality of a little girl. Betty also wore braces on her legs, so there were some physical deficits as well. I believe I heard that the dad, in this situation, could not handle the devastation of his daughter's injuries and abandoned the family. Mom spent her life caring for and sharing her life with this child. It always made me sad when this mom and daughter came into our office. I would see this old gray-haired woman and wonder, was that going to be me someday? But I realize that I had no idea what home life was like for either Betty or Dennis. Perhaps their parents got tired and frustrated like I did. Maybe they had several people who shared in their care. I just didn't know.

A television show I watched the other night gave me more to think about on this subject of parenting a special-needs child. The show was about conditions that have kept a person from growing. One family had a five-year-old daughter who was as small as a three-month-old baby. She drank formula from a bottle and just did not grow, either physically or mentally. Her condition was being contrasted and compared to that of a forty-year-old man who, despite the telltale wrinkles of forty-year-old skin, looked and acted like a nine-year-old. He, too, never grew in physical size or mental capacity. The parents of the little girl had three other young school-age children and simply toted their little infant five-year-old with them everywhere.

I felt sadness for this family because I know what it's going to feel like as they watch their other children grow and reach milestones while their special child simply stays put in her own special world. It's easy to include her in with other family activities because she's small and very portable. Life is busy with helping little ones dress, cutting their food, and helping them wash and learn new skills. This special daughter just needed extra help. Besides, she was little and cute. What were they going to do when the other children were grown and off to college? Twenty years later, when you are still diapering and feeding your twenty-five-year-old daughter, it is not so cute anymore.

On the other hand, the family of the forty-year-old man had finally decided to find a home for their son. They visited him often, both the parents and the siblings. Everyone had his or her own lives. This young man appeared happy and comfortable in his home. Mom appeared calm and confident when she visited her son. I wish I could talk to this mom to find out how she felt after finding a home for her son, and how long it took her to do it.

Throughout the years, it was always so nice to talk to other caregiving moms. Whether our children were still babies, school age, or young adults, there were always notes to share and compare. There was also a comfortable ease to our conversations, as we were both aware of the tremendous struggles and challenges we each faced. It was a little bit of the "I know how you feel" that I so desperately needed to hear.

Finding other families today with similar caregiving needs is easier than it was for me when Amanda was young. Besides the TOTE moms, the moms of other special ed classmates, or families from the spina bifida group that we met with occasionally, we had very little contact with families like ours. We were and are the minority. People today are very fortunate to have the Internet to make connections and interact with support groups. And although they may not live physically nearby, the amazing Internet can connect everybody and draw them into a common site. When you are connected with people and can share cheers and challenges, it makes coping with your caregiving situation a lot more bearable.

43
"God, Help Me": A Journaling Snapshot of Life with Amanda

When I stop to think about yesterday, or last week, or last year, or even the last twenty-nine years, I am amazed. There have been so many blessings, as well as painful challenges. I can't believe we've come this far. The road itself, if I could have had someone map it out for me, has been unbelievable, with many twists and turns that would seem humanly impossible. If I had known how steep, rocky, frightening, or painful parts of the road were going to be, I would have totally chosen to pick a different route. Who in his or her right mind would willingly choose such a rough and raw, unchartered pathway of life? Only in hindsight can I now look back and realize how faithful God has been to see me through. There were so many times I had to draw on His strength to simply make it through one more day. I know He helped me through. I believe He carried me some days.

Throughout the months and years that God has guided me through the writing of this book, I have found times that the writing came easily as well as times when the words flowed slowly and painfully. The "slow" times were when I struggled for the right phrasing or words to describe exactly what I wanted to share. The "painful" parts were those times when I reminisced and relived events and found myself reduced to tears. Some of my best writing times have been when I prayerfully found myself in a quiet spot, undistracted, with God directing the words as they flowed from my head, down my arms, to my fingertips and onto the keys of my computer. I have also had many writing times when life with Amanda became so scary or overwhelming that I turned to journaling my feelings just so I wouldn't burst from the pressure of the exploding emotions. Life with Amanda has been one of those proverbial roller-coaster rides. Many times I believed all the ups and downs, twists and turns, had rendered me quite loopy! There have been joys, accomplishments, blessings, miracles, and so many happy days. But the down days have included so much pain, sadness, fear, and disappointment. It is to God I give all the credit for guiding me through such a carnival lifestyle. To give you an idea of how painful the "down" days were, following are a few entries that I wrote when I was feeling desperate and just had to pour out my feelings. My journaling presented below is raw and unedited.

December 6, 2009. I've been going crazy with Christmas shopping this past week and have about 75 percent of it done. Just finished the Christmas cards today, including a family letter and photograph taken at Thanksgiving. The cards got dropped off in the mail this evening. I even started putting the tree up today. God dropped a thought into my head yesterday as I was frolicking in all the Christmas busy-ness. He told me that "this could be the last Christmas you celebrate with Amanda." The thought hit me hard and touched my heart while burning into my soul. Suddenly, I realized that the time spent with Amanda better be the best—for it might be the last.

This evening, Amanda started feeling sick and was puking everything she swallowed. The typical shaking and chills was happening again, and you could tell that she just felt miserable. Fear clutched at my heart and panic washed over me. As I look at her and how fragile she appears, and hear her puke and wretch as though she were turning inside out, it makes me cry out to God in agonizing frustration. My poor Amanda has been so bored lately, with so few friends. The cold temperatures outside creep in, and she is always cold, always combating cold hands and body. And when this unexplainable sickness hits her, I just want to cry out to God to take her home. In heaven she'll never be cold. In heaven she will never be lonely and will always have someone to talk to. In heaven, she will be running and skipping and able to reach everything. And then my insides knot up as my heart squeezes in pain as I think that I couldn't possibly imagine life without her. The tears are flowing fast for me, and the headache that started this morning has now intensified to a horrific throb. My only response to this agony is to say, over and over, "Thy will, Lord, not mine. Thy will, Lord, not mine."

My prayers over the years have always been that God will direct Ted and me to be the best parents we can be to Amanda and to make the best decisions for her. I pray for strength and peace and wisdom. That little girl has made me crazy over the years—crazy with love, crazy with frustration, crazy with pain. And as sick and sore and tired as I have been of taking care of her lately, it's just been a real chore to say "I love you" to her. She always says it to Ted and everyone else. It's not something I say all the time. I feel like it's overused and if you say it all the time, it loses its intensity. It's just not special if it's said all the *time. When Amanda says, "I love you" to me, I usually respond with either a "yeah" or "sleep good." Tonight I made a point of responding to her "I love you" at bedtime with "I love you, too."*

Monday morning, January 25, 2010. I slept horribly last night. Didn't get to bed until 11:30 and tossed and turned for half an hour before dozing off. Was awake and had to use the bathroom at 2:00 a.m. before putting myself back in bed and attempting to fall asleep again. This time, I woke up at 4:00 a.m. I woke up from a dream and was having a minor panic attack. Like most dreams, I could only remember the very last part of it. I was sitting on the couch with someone next to me. I can't remember who it was, but I think it was my friend Florence. We were sharing a large photo album on our laps between us and were looking at pictures of Amanda as a baby. Amanda had died. I leaned into my friend sitting next to me while gazing at a picture of a smiling, laughing, baby Amanda and said, "I can't believe she's gone."

Between the shock of the dream and the panic attack, I could not stay in bed. Grabbing a blanket from the linen closet, I went to lie down on the couch. Of course, I first tiptoed past Amanda's room to listen and make sure she was breathing. Lying on the couch, I wondered why I had such a dream. All I could figure was that it was God, again, tapping me on the shoulder to hurry up and finish this book. A little reminder and a prod that time may be short. It scares me to think about it.

Sunday evening, January 31, 2010. Tomorrow I leave for Grandville to visit Kristen and Jillian. I haven't seen them since Christmas. Ted doesn't mind if I go see them without him. It's easier without him because if he goes with me, it means making arrangements for someone to stay here with Amanda. That takes lots of planning and extra money. Besides, he has a lot of work to keep him busy anyway. So, of course, Amanda seemed a little "weird" to me. I asked her if she was okay. She said she was cold and had a little headache. She gets to acting strange when her health is not quite perfect—hard to describe, but I've seen enough over twenty-six years to know when something is a little off. Cold means chills, which means fever ... but she doesn't have a fever. Headache can mean anything from sinus issues to shunt problems. Of course, it may be that the house is just cold (it is) and she has a plain old headache. But she starts to sit funny, and she tips her head back and sideways. I just know something is "off." I ask her what I can do, and we decide that maybe a little medicine for the headache would help. So I give her some and I wait.

My stomach grows queasy as I start to worry about tomorrow and leaving. Part of me grows angry as I just wish I could have one day without worrying about her. It is such a feeling of bondage to feel forever trapped in this bubble of constant fear. I can't leave without making sure all is well here. I worry if she'll really start acting sick for Ted. He's not so good at handling some things. He needs me here, and I don't want him alone with a sick Amanda. I ache for release from this constant, gnawing threat of sickness and yearn for freedom. If only Ted and I could run away to some tropical island and relax in the sun, with no worries. So, the medicine seems to have made things a bit better, and she seems to just be tired. As she gets ready for bed, I sit here typing. God tapped me on my shoulder again and said to write.

Saturday evening, February 6, 2010. This evening Amanda decided that her stomach wasn't feeling well. She was cold (and the house was cold—the furnace had been accidentally bumped and turned down) and was wheeling laps around the house. She often would do laps as a sort of exercise, mainly for the purpose of getting her body warm. The next thing I heard, she was in the drawer taking out the digital thermometer and taking her temperature. That's not a good sign. Whenever Amanda doesn't feel good, she assumes that she has a fever—because a fever means you're sick. Well, she didn't have a fever. I asked what was wrong, and she told me that she didn't think the rice and baked beans she ate at dinner were making her stomach happy. It wasn't long after that when she suddenly got real big eyes and started wheeling frantically toward the cupboard with the plastic bowls in it. I got to the cupboard before her and took out one of the plastic bowls we use to catch her puke. And then she heaved and coughed and gagged. I have no idea why this wave of nausea hit her. It happened two times this past week as well. What makes her sick like this? What is going on in her tiny little body?

Sunday morning, February 7, 2010. I was hoping to wake up and find Amanda had recovered overnight. Doesn't a good night's sleep fix everything? And she had slept through the night just fine. But, she is sitting at the kitchen table and telling me she doesn't feel good. That she feels yucky all over. In my attempts to "fix" what's wrong, we run through the symptoms. She had already taken her temperature, and it was 97 something. All right, that's a little cold. Obviously, she doesn't have a fever. I ask her if she has a headache. "No," she answers. We check her heart rate and oxygen sats again, and they are both normal. Considering that she threw up before going to bed last night and hadn't touched the juice Ted had poured for her this morning, I tell her to drink. I figure she could be dehydrated or her blood sugar could be way low. She says "okay." I sit and watch her. Lips are pink. Everything is fine—at least for symptoms I can see. She still hasn't taken a drink, and I tell her that. I suggest that she's running on an empty stomach and remind her that the last time she was in the hospital, it was because she had a bad infection and had gotten dehydrated. I needed her to drink to see if it was going to make her feel better or simply make her puke. Either way, at least we were moving in one direction or another. She was going to start feeling better, or maybe I could call her sickness the flu. She ends up downing practically the whole glass of juice and a few crackers. Oh boy—I'm sure the puke is coming.

Ted has showered and is getting ready to go to church. I don't have to sing at any services today, but he has to play trumpet at the first two services. Amanda and I were going to join him at the second service. I am scared to take a shower in fear that she's going to throw up any minute. I tell Ted that Amanda and I will stay home from church today. He doesn't argue. We are both baffled. As I sit typing this on the computer, Amanda is now in her room and has turned on her computer. There is a portable heater in her room that we use to keep her room warm for her, and I turned it on high about ten minutes ago. She hasn't thrown up yet and has gone to check her e-mail in her warm room. We're making progress toward feeling better. But I still don't know. Something is just not right. There's something "off." There is this lump of uneasiness in my stomach that feels like a greasy, pulsing dense nugget of fear.

Same day, 9:30 a.m. I'm still afraid to shower. I just finished getting Amanda dressed for the day. Everything physical that I can see is okay. But she's just not right. I hate this feeling. I hate living like this. Life revolves around Amanda's needs and how *she is feeling. Her health can change from good to bad overnight. And we aren't always sure what's going on. It feels like being in prison sometimes to me. Forgive me for turning this around to a "feel sorry for Laurel" thing, but it's how I feel. Amanda's needs are always there, and someone has to do the job. Every morning I have two bodies to get ready for the day. I wonder what it will feel like when she's gone and I only have one person to get ready. Will I feel relief or release from the twenty-six years of service to her, or will I miss it and feel lost?*

44
Caregiver Duty 24/7: A Journaling Snapshot of Extreme Caregiving—or How I Almost Lost My Mind

Currently, at the writing of this chapter, I am living alone with Amanda in our Trenton house. Ted was offered a job in the Chicago area, and until we can sell our house, I am here and he is there. My worst fear has been realized. I am alone in the care of my daughter.

The journal entries following begin with Ted interviewing for the job that would move him to Indiana, away from me and Amanda. Thus begins the period of time of my worst fear realized.

Friday, February 19, 2010. Ted went to Chicago and back yesterday for a job interview. He has been his own boss and running his own business since he lost his job some nine years ago. We've been getting by and managing pretty well. But this is a really good job opportunity for Ted. It would mean us moving to the Chicago area. I have such mixed feelings. If we didn't have

Amanda to worry about, it would be simple. I could go with Ted, and we could take our time finding just the right house. It would be a great adventure finding new places to shop, picking a new church, and making new friends. But Amanda makes none of this easy. Amanda grew up in this area, and we have twenty-six years of history with doctors and other medical services.

House hunting alone would be a challenge. Do I leave her here with a sitter each time I go west to house hunt with Ted? Or do I drag her along each time? If Ted takes the job, they will want him working there within two weeks, so we are already resigned to the fact that he will have to go ahead of me and start working. I will have to stay here and keep working at my job and try to get our house sold. I am dreading the weeks I will spend, just Amanda and me. Ted is my relief when I grow weary of taking care of Amanda. If he leaves, I will have to be her caregiver twenty-four seven. I think I may go crazy.

The town Ted will be working in is right on the northern tip of Indiana, sandwiched right in between the state of Illinois to the west, and Michigan to the east. Do I check out each state as to which one has the best services available for Amanda? And how do I find doctors for her? Do we choose a place close to a medical center? How do I arrange for her to get medical supplies? These are all tough things to carry out. Everything before just fell into place because we've lived in the same place all these years and we just kept riding that conveyor belt that was part of the system for handicapped individuals here in southeast Michigan. And then, I am also thinking that maybe this is a good time to get Amanda moved out of our home. How do I find alternative living situations for her? It would be wonderful to move her into a group home that was close to our new home. Relief at last! It would be a new life for Amanda as well. There is so much to consider, so many questions and so many fears.

Yesterday there was a young twenty-three-year-old girl in our city who passed away. She was a friend of a friend of my daughter Jillian. This poor girl had just graduated from nursing school and was getting ready to take the state test to become a licensed nurse when she fell ill. She ended up being diagnosed with an aggressive form of brain cancer. Nine months after being diagnosed, this poor young, vibrant, and energetic girl had to say good-bye to this world. She never had the chance to work as a nurse, to love and marry, to have a family of her own, and to live a full life. Her parents, naturally, were heartbroken, as well as so many friends and family members. I cried as I read all the comments people wrote on her obituary website.

There are just so many instances when I have observed a death of a young daughter, or mother, or child, and I want to ask God, "Why?" If He needed someone new in heaven on that day, why did he take someone with so much potential and life in them? Here I have my poor broken Amanda, who struggles every day for health and comfort, and He takes someone home with Him who really still had a lot of potential and responsibilities here on earth. I mentioned this to my daughter Jillian last night. Jillian commented that God must still need to use Amanda here on this earth. Her job must not be done yet. Well, what was this other girl's job that she was done already? Dear God, I am just so tired. All I want is for Amanda to be happy and to thrive. *That's always been the word I say to God when I pray for Amanda. Dear God, please allow Amanda to* thrive. *Instead, I feel like each day is a struggle for her as she accomplishes little or nothing while I worry about her and my joints ache from lifting and caring for her. The only thing that keeps me going is the faith that God has a plan bigger than I can imagine. His timing is perfect. He is my strength to get me through another day. Why? I don't know. And so my list of "why's" just gets bigger as I take God's hand and walk through this day, knowing that someday I'll have all the answers to my "why's." Proverbs 3:6, Trust in the Lord with all your heart and lean not on your own understanding.*

Tuesday, June 29, 2010. I cannot believe it's been over four months since my last entry. On the one hand, it is a very good thing because I have not had to write about Amanda being sick. Funny, I can't even remember the last time she threw up. Her health has been quite good and stable. Perhaps it is because Amanda no longer attends school? It would make sense that her susceptibility to being ill would lessen as we keep her away from a crowded, germ-filled environment like school. Oh, she's had a couple of urinary tract infections, but nothing too serious and nothing that a round of antibiotics couldn't clear up. But on the other hand, I have not written because life has been incredibly busy. Ted took the job in the Chicago area. His office is actually in Crown Point, Indiana. It is a four-hour car ride across the state of Michigan and into Indiana to get there. The house has been up for sale for three months now. I spend my days keeping the house looking good for the occasional potential buyer and real estate person to come take a look. Besides that, I take care of Amanda. Ted lives in a temporary apartment in Indiana and we see each other on weekends. It's been challenging.

I have made several trips to Indiana with Amanda in tow. Each time we go, I have to pack her clothes, her sleeping bag and pillow, her catheters and pee stuff, her potty seat and poop stuff, and her bi-pap machine. There's so much to pack! Then I get to load her and all her stuff in the van, along with my one little bag, and drive to Ted's apartment, only to unload everything when I get there.

It is because of Amanda that this move for Ted and me has become quite frustrating and difficult. On one of our visits to Ted in Indiana, Amanda and I went to one of the state offices that handle services for the developmentally disabled. We had already filled out the extensive application and were now taking part in the personal interview. This meeting would then set Amanda up for various special services available for the disabled in Indiana, including housing, respite care, day programs, and work programs. Several weeks after our extensive interview, I received a letter that stated Amanda had been put on a waiting list! I then found out that the state still had applications to process from eight years ago! Our letter further explained how we were to inform the state of any changes in Amanda's status or address and that we had to stay in touch once a year to keep our application on file. So, here was Ted with a promising new job in a new state, and the state had absolutely nothing to offer Amanda.

Moving to Indiana would mean giving up all that she was getting from Michigan. Even more specifically, the state of Michigan has a "home care" program that allows handicapped and elderly individuals to choose who they want as their caregivers, and arrange for them to be compensated by the state. The idea behind the program is that it allows special-needs individuals to stay at home in their own familiar surroundings with family or friends instead of institutionalizing them. It saves the state money, and these individuals are given the care they need. I am Amanda's paid caregiver. I know it sounds strange, because I'm her mom and that's my job, right? I was actually offered to be part of this program for many years, and I always turned it down because I just didn't feel right being paid to take care of my own daughter. It was only a couple years ago that I finally joined.

Ted had lost his job in 2001, and we had many rough years where he was running his own business while we struggled with keeping up with the bills and putting the two other daughters through college. Money was tight, the children were leaving the nest, and yet we had Amanda home with us still, challenging us both physically and monetarily. I finally decided to accept the assistance from this program to make life a little easier for Amanda, and to feel somewhat rewarded and compensated for the daily, continuous care I give her. On the days where I just don't feel like taking care of her anymore, it helps somewhat to know that there is a financial reward for the whole family for what I do. The program pays based on how much time is spent each day to take care of a patient's needs. Amanda needs lots of physical care. The checks helped.

The bottom line problem is that Indiana does not have a program like this. So, for us to move to Indiana, we would have no special-needs services for her until our application goes through—and who knows when that will be! We would have to give up the Michigan home care program as well. And even if we do get services in Indiana, there is no compensation program for caregivers. So now we don't know what to do! We have considered moving to the very southwestern edge of Michigan near the Indiana border so that Amanda can receive state of Michigan benefits, but the cost would be a forty-five minute to an hour commute for Ted to work. It's doable, I guess. It's also a better drive than the four-hour drive that separates us now! But it is just so frustrating to not know where to move to right now, all for the sake of making the best decision for Amanda.

Another option that we are considering is perhaps it is time for us to find a home for Amanda. I am searching out options for her both in Michigan and Indiana. I heard that if we found a group home with an opening for Amanda in Indiana, that the money would quickly become available. Wonder how that suddenly works? If we find a place for her in Michigan, the home care money I get would then transfer to that home, and that would be fine. To move Amanda out to a group home, separate from Ted and me, is a terrifying decision for me. Of course, I believe that there is no one better to take care of her than Ted or me. Haven't Ted and I been the ones to notice when her health wasn't great, to the point of literally saving her life at times? I am so scared that she won't be watched, won't be cared for, won't be happy, and won't be loved. But I am so tired—how can I keep taking care of her? To let her live somewhere else now makes me nauseous. What if? And what if?

With all the unknowns in the Greshel family right now, I have found that I can do little more than pray to God for peace and direction. Our house is not selling, and we don't know where to move. I truly believe God has a plan for us. I simply have no idea what that plan is.

Sunday, July 11, 2010. It's probably nothing, but I got this "mom" feeling about Amanda that something is off with her today. As usual, she was up before me today. I, myself, have not been sleeping well at all lately, and am usually awake by 5:30 and, because I can't fall back asleep, am up out of bed by 6:00 a.m. Today, I dozed until almost 7:00 a.m., and Amanda was up already. Not sure what time she gets up and out of bed. Most mornings I am up by 6:00 a.m., and she is already up with the television on. So, who knows how early she is really getting out of bed. Off to 9:45 church we went after washing, dressing, and eating breakfast. Amanda sat to my right at the end of the pew in the central aisle at church. I turned to her to whisper something, and she turned toward me but her eyes were all over the place. It is not unusual for her eyes to twitch some. It's as though she is trying to look at you and her eyes keep jerking off to the side. I've seen this occasionally, and so it is usually no big deal. But this morning her eyes were twitching all over the place, and I had to tell Amanda to, literally, look at me. With concentration, she looked at me, although her eyes still quivered some.

After we got home from church, Amanda just seemed melancholy. I kept asking her if she was okay, and she kept telling me that she was. It's as though she was depressed and withdrawn. And very tired as well. I know she is scared and sad about moving. I just don't know.

Life has been such a jumble of emotions lately. I am lonely for my husband, who has been working in another state for four months now. The weeks get long and boring, and then when he comes home for a weekend, it is a flurry of activity. He leaves, and the boredom starts again. For the days that it is just Amanda and me, I feel rather like a slave. My day is built around Amanda's needs. I've been taking care of Amanda for over twenty-six years now.

Tuesday, August 3, 2010. Today is Amanda's birthday. I am crying. Ted continues to live and work in Indiana while I sit in our for-sale house in Trenton, Michigan. I told Ted last night that I many times have lusted for the divorced lifestyle that would give me every other weekend or even every other week without kids. I never dreamed I'd get exclusive custody. I told him, again, how tired I am and how I rarely get a break. He responded, "Do you think I haven't thought of that?" It helps just to know that he thinks about it, too. He knows I am struggling.

I should be all cheerful and excited for Amanda. She still treats birthdays as if she were five years old. She wants a party, streamers, and balloons, with presents everywhere and guests galore. I remind her that she is now twenty-seven, and it's time she should stop recognizing her birthday so obviously to everyone. A woman, sooner or later, has to start fibbing about her age. But she has been telling everyone for a month now that August 3 is her birthday. Just like any other little kid. Oh, we will celebrate. I will take her to the store today to pick out a cake of her choice. She really likes choosing from the case filled with sugary cakes and swirling frosting flowers of all colors. I bought her a really cool present that I will wrap and surprise her with later. And I am treating her to a haircut this afternoon. I am even letting her get a streak of purple hair dye in her hair. She thinks that is so cool. But I feel so guilty because I don't want to celebrate. I am so tired of taking care of her. All this birthday stuff just adds to what I have to do. I know it sounds selfish, hence, my guilt feelings. But when you are tired from all that you do for someone, and then you have to do more, well, you just don't want to!

Tuesday, August 3, 2010. Later on this same day … It's been a nice day. Amanda and I met my parents at a local deli for lunch. [Laurel's parents moved to Michigan from Kentucky in 2005.] *We told Amanda she was getting a lunch out for her birthday, and Grandma topped it off with a birthday card and check for Amanda. After lunch, I took Amanda to the grocery store to choose a cake. Of course, she picked one with confetti sprinkles and purple icing. Our next stop was the hair salon. God bless Ashleigh, the hair stylist who is so patient with Amanda. Ashleigh is very cool, with two-toned hair that is partially shaved off on one side. She helped Amanda choose a nice style haircut and added some well-placed purple highlights in Amanda's hair. The whole time, Ashleigh and Amanda chatted about all kinds of things. Amanda loved the attention. When we got home, I immediately took pictures of Amanda's new haircut and color and posted them for her on Facebook. Amanda's been thoroughly enjoying all the birthday cards in the mail, the Facebook posts on the computer, and the attraction her posted pictures have provided. Everyone is commenting to her on her purple hair. Now that Jill is home from work, we are going to do cake and presents next. I hope she's enjoyed her birthday.*

Tuesday, October 26, 2010. Time has flown by! Jillian got married on October 2, and obviously, there was much to do in the weeks prior to her wedding date. Ted is working in Indiana, and Amanda and I are still in the Trenton house.

Wednesday, November 3, 2010. Amanda is sick, and I feel sucked empty of all my being. It has been almost eight months since Ted has gone to Indiana to work. The house is still for sale. I miss Ted, and I am tired. The responsibilities are overwhelming, and I feel like I just put myself on autopilot each day, just to get through. If I let down my guard and open my mind to things, I start losing it and the tears start. Better to stay numb and keep plowing through the day.

After I put Amanda to bed two nights ago, she got up about twenty minutes later and wheeled into the living room. I asked her what was wrong. She said she wanted to check on her heater and get a drink. Amanda gets obsessed with making sure what setting the heater is on. But I also knew that she took a long nap earlier in the day, so I questioned her about perhaps not being tired due to her long nap. I also wondered if she didn't feel well, and she told me she was fine. I finally put her back to bed, and she slept the rest of the night. The next morning, she woke up at her usual 6:00 a.m. As the morning progressed, she informed me that she didn't feel well. We checked her heart rate and her oxygen sats and those were fine, meaning we weren't dealing with a respiratory infection or pneumonia. She said she was cold and sweaty and just felt yucky all over. Oh boy, here we go again. I mentioned the night before, and she admitted she hadn't felt good then, either. I wish she would tell me the truth when I ask her. Fortunately, I was able to get her into the doctor's in the afternoon, and it looks like another urinary tract infection. After getting two doses of medicine into her before bedtime, I put her to bed and prayed we caught things in time and with the right antibiotic.

This morning after she woke up, she puked. Oh, great. So now I have her dosed up on acetaminophen and am praying the antibiotic kicks in soon. Of course, I am trying to get away for a night this weekend, so why wouldn't Amanda get sick? Instead of either one of us driving all the way to the other's place this weekend, Ted and I thought we'd meet in the middle in Grand Rapids and stay the night in a hotel. I have a new girl staying with Amanda here at the house. Ted and I didn't even see each other last weekend, and we are anxious to get together this weekend. My daughter Kristen will be in Grand Rapids as well, and Ted and I were hoping for a night away and some time with our other daughter.

It is at times like this that I fear we will never get Amanda moved out somewhere else. Who else would have noticed that she was sick as soon as I did?

November 4, 2010. I am too tired to cry. I was tired yesterday. I told God that I feel broken. Like a rag doll that has been torn open and all its stuffing pulled out, I feel like a puddle of worn-out old fabric in a small heap on the floor. Amanda came to my room last night at 2:15 a.m. to say that she had thrown up. She proceeded to throw up two more times. I haven't been back to bed since 2:15. I have taken my shower and sit here typing while she is resting at the table in the kitchen. During the day, Amanda will lay her head down on the kitchen table to take a little nap instead of lying down on her bed or the couch. She prefers it. But I am so tired I feel sick to my stomach and the chest pains were starting. I am not having a heart attack, but rather, it is the chest pains that come from stress. They are recognizable to me from previous experiences. The fatigue has made me numb, and yet I have this weird calmness about me.

The past months feel like such a test to me. Why God is testing me, I do not know. But it feels like Satan would love for me to lose my patience and lose control so that I can get angry with God and look for relief from the devil himself. I can almost feel the evil trying to creep into my soul as I cope with my challenging situation right now, and I have had to tell Satan to flee! My house is home to Jesus, and the devil is not welcome here! Satan will not win. I truly feel that God intervened by giving me the intuition to get Amanda to the doctor's early on Tuesday. I believe we caught this infection just in time to keep it from going systemic and landing her in the hospital. I am peacefully optimistic that things will turn around today and she'll start feeling better.

Ted and I need some time this weekend, and I believe God knows that. And my daughter Kristen deserves our attention this weekend as well. She has been the least dependent on Ted and me over the years, and it will be wonderful to spend some time with her. My poor middle child! Her older sister, Amanda, has had most of the attention over the years. And her younger sister, Jillian, besides being the baby of the family, just had six months of attention leading up to her wedding day. It's Kristen's turn! God has control over all of this, and I wait patiently for all things to work out.

Tuesday, November 9, 2010. Last week's medicine worked, and Ted and I got away for a night this past weekend. Thank you, God!

Wednesday, November 10, 2010. I find it pitiful that the only way I can describe how I feel lately is "I'm tired." I am tired of taking care of Amanda, tired of having my husband living and working in another state, tired of not getting enough sleep, and just tired of my life. I wish I could sleep for just six hours straight at night. What a miracle that would be! Oh, it would probably be better if I could get the recommended eight hours, or even seven, but six would be a great improvement right now. My first challenge to sleep had been to adjust to sleeping alone since Ted is gone. I think I'm getting used to that by now. Of course, my second challenge is Amanda. At this time, it has become the evening routine that I make a bedtime call to Ted so just the two of us can talk without Amanda wanting to take a turn.

Wednesday, December 8, 2010. I got my hair cut and the gray covered up yesterday. The gray roots were showing, and I had too much hair all over the place. After the hair color was brushed on, I had to sit for about half an hour while the dye soaked in. It is a very unflattering look to have one's hair painted and plastered with hair dye. I tried to keep my nose buried in the well-worn magazines that are always abundant in hair salons. At one point, I dared to look up at my reflection in the mirror and was shocked at what I saw. Oh, the hair was wild, with the roots plastered to my head with thick sticky hair dye, and the rest of it wild and sticking out every which way. That part I expected to see. But my face is what startled me. I realize that I am getting older, but what I saw scared me. I looked so very tired, with dark circles under my eyes. There was very little color in my face, and I looked almost pasty. And I looked sad.

It's been a year since I started journaling this part of the book. It's been nine months since Ted has been living and working in Indiana, leaving Amanda and me here in Trenton. Physically and emotionally, I feel like I am falling apart. It seems to be worse as the weather gets colder. I keep Amanda dressed in three shirts: a long-sleeved thermal top, a turtleneck, and then either a fleece shirt or sweater on top. Numerous times each day, I hear Amanda in her bathroom warming herself up with her blow dryer. It drives me crazy. I cannot turn the heat up any higher because our heating bills are already outrageous. I've encouraged Amanda to move so she can create some of her own body heat since all she really does is sit around all day. Of course, she'll be cold. But I also worry that her little body just isn't keeping up, and the sound of the blow dryer frustrates me as much as it scares me.

Yesterday morning I felt like I was having a heart attack. I was almost thinking of calling the doctor. My heart was racing, and I could feel my whole body pulse with the beating of my heart. I was nauseous, and my chest ached. I chalked it up to stress and the side effects I sometimes experience after taking my morning vitamin. After that scare yesterday morning and my shocked reaction to the reflection I saw in the salon mirror, I was hoping for a restful night and a better morning today. That didn't happen.

At 2:30 a.m. I at first thought that the cat was knocking at my closed bedroom door. The cat can be a nuisance at night when he decides to get in bed and either lick your face or attack your feet through the covers, hence the closed door. The knocking was from Amanda. I shot out of bed to open the door, and asked her what she was doing up at 2:30. She replied that she had woken up and her stomach was upset. She had gotten out of bed because she thought she was going to throw up. Out of my extreme fatigue, I started crying and asked her what were we going to do now that we were all wide awake at 2:30 in the morning, including a cat who thought it was wonderful that everyone was available to play. Amanda's "sick" feeling quickly disappeared, and because I think she knew I was tired and upset, she asked me to put her back in bed. Crying, I lifted her out of her wheelchair for the second time that night to lay her down in bed, with my tired arms hurting again with lifting her weight.

After tucking her in and getting all the covers pulled up just right, I closed her bedroom door and contemplated my choices for getting more sleep. If I went back to bed and closed my door, I would risk not hearing Amanda if she called, and I would most certainly hear the cat howl outside my door. He was wide-awake and knew I was as well. As far as he was concerned, it was playtime. If I kept my door open, the cat in his playful mood would be all over the dressers and getting into everything he could, including the covers and me. I opted to grab a big blanket and lay on the couch. I could hear Amanda from the couch in the family room, and I was hoping the cat would settle down to whatever he did when I closed him out of my bedroom at night. Amanda never called out, and although the cat tried to play a little, he chose to snuggle up with my big warm blanket and me. I barely got any sleep. It was nice to have a slumbering kitty join me on the couch, but he kept me from being able to move around much, as he was sleeping so tight up against me.

After a little bit of dozing, I ended up with my hips aching from my recent bursitis attacks, and my head and neck were stiff from trying to sleep on a throw pillow. Finally, at 5:00 a.m., I stumbled in pain and with a headache to my bed, and closed the door behind me. I immediately heard the howling protests of the cat outside my closed door, wondering why I had abandoned him. But I was too tired to care. I believe I dozed for about forty-five minutes before getting up at 6:00 a.m. to seek the healing comforts of a hot cup of coffee. I found Amanda already up and watching TV.

Although I try hard not to "lose it," I lost it in front of Amanda this morning. I started crying again and asked her if she knew how tired I was. I asked her what she thought of me having to get up in the middle of the night with a twenty-seven-year-old, and rather accused her of being a big baby. I let off a bit of steam, and even cursed a few times before putting the lid back on my explosive frustrations and reining myself in. I know it's not fair to unload my feelings on Amanda. She's not normal. She doesn't understand fully. It makes her feel horrible, and then that makes me feel more horrible as well when I see that I've upset her. But I can only take so much, and I have no one else to unload on.

Saturday, December 18, 2010. If hope is like a bubble, than I have a puddle of burst bubbles, like tears, at my feet. For nine months, Ted has lived in another state, and I have been here with Amanda. I miss my husband. I am suffocating under the constant care of Amanda. There have been so many "hopes" over the past months. Like little teasing bubbles that suddenly appear as glistening, perfect, little shiny orbs. They bring delight with their appearance. Each bubble brings the hope of a possible new thing for this family. Every showing of our house brings the hope of a buyer. We've even had a land contract deal that almost worked out, and even a cash offer on our house that, unfortunately, didn't amount to enough cash. I have made countless phone calls and e-mail contacts with people and organizations that might help with finding a new home for Amanda. Every one sounded exciting, and my bubble of hope would grow bigger. Nine months later, we have made no progress. Every bubble of hope that might bring a sale of our house or a solution for Amanda has burst. The puddle at my feet is huge, like a warm, salty lake of tears.

Sunday, January 9, 2011. The past three weeks flew past. The best part is that Ted was home for ten days between Christmas and New Year's. We also had a visit from both Jillian and Andy, and Kristen and Ric. Now the tree and all decorations are packed away and everyone has gone home, leaving me here alone with Amanda. We have sunk back into the same old daily routine. Life is boring. Doesn't help that it is so cold outside, but what do you expect for a Michigan winter? Amanda hates to be cold, so going anywhere with her is a challenge, if it happens at all. She has to bundle up so much, and then there's the lifting I do of her and her chair in the freezing outside. It's cold and it's not fun. Many times, she opts to not go if I am running to the store. I'm glad when she stays home because it spares my back and shoulders to not have to lift her, and I am out in the cold less. But then I feel bad for her all cooped up inside the house all of the time.

Yesterday, we drove to the mall so we could just get out of the house and go somewhere. The mall was a far enough drive away that the van had time to really warm up and crank out the heat before we got there. We walked the whole perimeter of the mall, stopping in a store or two that caught our attention. I didn't buy anything. An hour later, we drove home. At least we got out for a bit.

45

Sharing Caregiver Duties Once Again

It was a bit more than a year that I lived without Ted in our Michigan home. In hindsight, I see it as one of the hardest, loneliest, and darkest years of my life. On days when things seemed the most desperate, I would find myself singing "Breath of Heaven" by Amy Grant. The lyrics reflect what Jesus's mother probably felt as she got close to her son's birth. Young, pregnant, scared, unsure, and anxious about giving birth to God's son, Mary could only trust that God would be with her as she walked her path alone. On the days when fatigue ruled, emotions were raw, muscles ached, loneliness lingered, and the prayers of help could not be formed, I would simply close my eyes and hope that the simple air I felt on my face was God's presence. The breath of heaven. Too empty and spent to face another day, I would sing to God to please hold me together.

Monday, July 11, 2011. I don't know how the past six months got away from me without my writing. In hindsight, I think I was literally in "survival mode" and just trying to live and get by. The first three months of the year, Amanda and I continued our life of hibernation in the house as winter kept us inside. I recall those months as a smudge of days all smooshed together. Every day was pretty much the same as I took care of Amanda and the cat, while tending to the basic needs of keeping the house clean, feeding the three of us, and keeping the bills paid. As things slowly warmed into spring, we crawled out of hibernation. That and daughter Kristen's May 1 wedding gave us a task to stay busy with and, somehow, kept us sane. It was right around the time of Kristen's wedding when Ted decided that he had to come home. Our house hadn't sold, the anticipated new life in Indiana wasn't materializing, and Ted wanted and needed to come home to Michigan. So he did. Somehow God managed for a phone call to be made to Ted from an old acquaintance in the business world, and the pieces were put together over several weeks so that Ted could have a new job and be at home instead of living apart from us in Indiana. Amen!

July 26, 2011. A few weeks after Ted moved home, we had a little talk about how it was good to all be in the same home again. Ted commented on how he was so relieved to be home so he could help me with the house and Amanda. Knowing how much I had struggled over the past year, out of the blue I asked him this question: "Was I really that bad?" Ted understood the meaning of the question, as to how I was becoming a little unstable and burned-out. He replied, "Laurel, I had to come home—you were getting really bad." He said it hurt him to see me struggle; he would hear the strain and fatigue in my voice on the phone. I cried as I tried to recall the last several months, where life seemed like a numb blur. I continue to marvel at how God faithfully helped me through. Like the footprints in the sand poem, I can look back and see just one set of footprints. When I could no longer manage on my own, He carried me.

The whole family on New Year's Day, January 1, 2012.

46

Getting Back to a Sane Existence: Finding Out a "Why" to Amanda's Purpose

Things are back to being pretty much "same old" around here. I guess you could say we've settled into our own "normal" for now. It's me, Ted, and Amanda. We still live in the same house and on the same street as we establish the mundane routines of everyday life. A year ago, we were looking forward to a new home and community to live in. It was exciting to anticipate new friends, new shopping sites, and new places to dine. Amanda is still the same. She is who she is, with the same quirkiness. She has good days, and she has questionable days, where her color is not quite right and her physical health seems not so stable. Still, she thrives. Life goes on. There is even a strange peace in the familiarity of the "same old."

So what has changed in the past year? Amanda's two younger sisters are now married and living in their own homes. We feel that it's time now to change Amanda's address as well. Yes, Ted and I are scared. Of course, no one can take better care of her than us. We feel guilt as well.

It is simply through my faith in God's promise, "In all things God works for the good of those who love Him who have been called according to His purpose" (Rom 8:28), that I can go on each day. For whatever reason, God created Amanda. Sometimes I don't understand why or what purpose He has for her. Like many things in life, I don't expect to know the reason why, although I hope to when I get to heaven. The fact that she has survived so many medical scares simply amazes me, especially when I've been witness to so many who have died before her, and before their time. I am certain that I would be a different person today if it weren't for Amanda.

I hope my experiences through her and because of her have made me a better person. You might say I can see some things through different eyes, as I have had quite a different perspective at times. My faith has been challenged, my emotions strained and torn, my heart broken and hurt, my physical energy sucked dry, tears wept until I'm empty, and my life at times turned upside down. All those things have helped to shape me into who I am. Perhaps, like clay in the potter's hands, God is molding and shaping me? I know for certain that throughout everything, I have learned that there is nothing more important in life than the love of family and friends and the joy and peace that come from faith in God. You can strip me of all material things from my house to any jewels or things of value that I have, for they mean nothing in comparison to the precious love of others. Fancy cars, designer clothes, the latest electronic gadget, or the perfectly decorated room have no value when you are sitting at the hospital bedside of a sick daughter.

I am sure there have been people touched by Amanda's life. There is one person, in particular, that I know about and would like to share with you. Back in the spring of 1992, we were preparing ourselves for Amanda's big back surgery. This was the surgery that had me so frightened. It was May 28, a Thursday, and our church was celebrating the Ascension. The Ascension service is forty days after Easter and celebrates the risen Christ's return to heaven. The tradition at our church was to let go a bunch of helium balloons. Tied to each balloon was a card with the name of a child on it and a short message to the recipient about Jesus, and a request for a return reply as it was always fun to see whose balloon would travel the greatest distance. Sometimes we got no responses, and sometimes several. Responses would come from near and far. In 1992, only one response from a drifting balloon came back. Amanda's balloon had traveled almost two hundred miles to Elkhart, Indiana. Between the time Amanda let her balloon go on Ascension Thursday and getting the note from its recipient, Amanda had endured her surgery. She was still hospitalized and recovering when I got the postcard from Charles with this simple note:

Dear Amanda: Surprise … your balloon reached its destination— my front yard. Thank you for the encouragement that Jesus loves me. I need to hear that again & again. I grew up in Central Africa and am studying for the ministry. Blessings, Charles.

We were delighted that Amanda's balloon had traveled so far and had been found by a man of God. It seemed an important sign to us as we weathered and recovered from Amanda's great surgery. I quickly wrote a lengthy letter back to Charles and told him about Amanda and her recent surgical challenge. I shared how special it was that hers was the only balloon to get a response. Charles wrote back and told of how he had just graduated from seminary and was returning from a six-week honeymoon with his new wife. He went on in his letter to tell how the last three years had been difficult for him as he began to question God's faithfulness. He and his wife were at the crossroads of a big decision in life—to stay in the United States to pastor a congregation or to go overseas in mission work. After meeting one evening with their church's search committee, Charles wrote about what happened the morning of the day he received my lengthy letter:

Then this morning my wife and I spent time reading the story of Gideon and praying. Remember how Gideon put out a fleece? (Judges 6 36ff) As my wife and I prayed, we too put out a fleece asking God for a "sign." Then this afternoon, I opened your letter. As my wife and I read it, we began to weep. I'm not sure exactly why, but it spoke to us of God's gentle but strong presence. I suppose hearing of Amanda's courage to face the hardships she has had to, called me to face my fears and be courageous—to take courageous steps. Just this morning, I told my wife, "One thing I desire from God is courage, like Gideon, who faced his own weakness and the incredible odds but chose to trust and believe God." Your letter was an answer to my fleece, a message sent from God. So I guess the blessing goes both ways. Thanks so much! Charles.

That was the last I heard from Charles. I don't know what direction he took, but I know that God used Amanda and her situation to speak to him. How many others have been recipients of a message from God through what they've seen in Amanda?

Amanda, getting ready to release her balloon after the Ascension service. Sister Kristen is in the foreground, and younger sister Jillian is on the right in the striped dress. Amanda's balloon ended up traveling nearly two hundred miles.

I remember a lyric from a song back in my junior high school days. I was in the junior high choir, in the days when it was cool to have a choral group and we could even sing songs that were spiritual and not just secular. The lyric was: "Lord, make me an instrument of your peace on earth." I could even sing it for you today, as I remember the melody. This remembered melody plays in my head at times, especially when I need to try and understand my purpose on earth. The song makes me think how we are all instruments or tools, made by God and created for His purpose. Some of us are large, like a string bass or a powerful jackhammer, while others are small, like a piccolo or simply a drill bit. Some of us are loud, some soft. Some of us play a gentle tune or softly turn a screw, while others blare loudly as from a horn, or are powerful like a sledgehammer and can break down walls.

But if we succumb to God's will and let him use us for His purpose, we will be fulfilling our purposes. For some, our task is short and sweet. Others must toil at a larger task.

Ted and I have been blessed with each other and with the gift of three wonderful daughters. God has helped us through the years to raise them. Now, two of them are married adult women, who both love God and will be having families of their own to grow and nurture. I know that God has plans for all of them. It seems to still be part of God's plan for us to have Amanda. He must not be done with her yet. It has always been our prayer that God would guide Ted and me to be the best parents we can be, and especially to make the right decisions in regard to Amanda's care. Now that she is twenty-nine years old, we feel it is time to push the little bird out of the nest and give her wings. I pray every day for the next step in Amanda's life, and for God to help us find a new home for Amanda.

This book has been about the dark times and challenges in my twenty-nine years of caring for my daughter. I have shared with you my most private thoughts, which at times may have seemed cruel and raw. Please forgive my honesty. I also do not mean to offend anyone with using terms that may not be considered "politically correct." My daughter is handicapped. It sounds nice to say that she is handi-capable. I could just say that she is challenged. (But aren't we all?) She is also not made like the rest of us, so I even describe her as "broken." You can describe her any way you wish, but she is who she is. And with that thought, I have come to think that, perhaps, it is the rest of us and not Amanda who are broken.

I recall an incident that happened about two years ago. I was at the bowling alley with Amanda, where she was bowling with a large group of developmentally disabled adults. My daughter Jillian was with us. It was the summer before Jillian got married, and she was living at home at that time. She was taking a class in animal genetics and was sitting toward the back, where she could watch her sister bowl while studying at the same time. One of the bowlers walked past Jillian and tenderly reached out and closed her hand around a large section of Jill's thick, silky, long blonde hair. She gently pulled her hand away and let the soft hair slip through her grasped hand. With the sweetest smile on her face, this person looked at Jillian and said, "Pretty!" before continuing on her way. The whole event lasted not more than ten seconds, yet it was full of purity and simplicity as this person found such treasured delight in the touch, feel, and sight of Jillian's long blonde hair.

How often do most of us miss those wonderful small bits of joy in life because we are drowning in the hustle and bustle of this materialistic life? Jill and I talked about it later, especially how it was so ironic that Jill happened to be studying genetics at the time, albeit animal genetics and not human. But I am pretty sure that this person who touched Jill's hair had Down's syndrome. Genetically, Down's syndrome occurs when a person has an extra chromosome. Both Jill and I questioned if maybe the rest of us were actually missing a chromosome. What if all those with the extra chromosome were the perfect ones? There are a whole bunch of us ordinary creations, but few who were created special. While the majority of us live our lives with worries and stress, the few lucky other ones learn to live in simple joy.

It made me realize that God had created Amanda just the way he wanted her. As I struggled through the years with wishing and praying that she could do this or become that, I was forgetting the simple fact that God had created her and God's plan is perfect. So, for all I've learned and all I've become as Amanda's mom, for all the tears I've cried and challenges endured, I praise God for the road I've traveled and where I am today. I thank Him for my daughter Amanda, perfectly made.

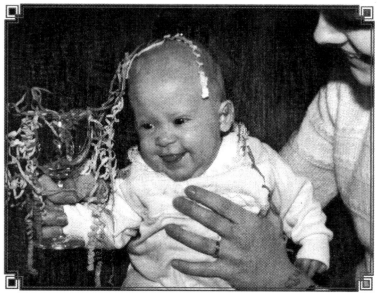

Amanda, January 1, 1984, joyfully celebrating her first New Year's.

Acknowledgments

Romans 11:36
For from him and through him and for him are all things. To him be the glory forever! Amen.

From God, I have received the love and support of my family, which made the writing of this book possible. Thank you, Mom and Pop, for taking me to church as a child, encouraging my creativity, instilling the value of education, and molding me into who I have grown up to be. Thank you, Theodore, for encouraging my writing while continuing to be the most loving, supportive, faithful, and unbelievable husband ever. To my daughters Kristen and Jillian, I thank you for all the joy you supply me and for all of your encouraging phone calls where you asked, "How's the book coming?" And thank you, Amanda, for giving me a story to share.

Through God, I have been privileged to be in contact with so many people who helped with this project. Thank you, Doug and Margaret, for reading my early manuscript and giving me affirmation to pursue publishing. Thank you, Leah, that I could trust you with valuable early review and editing. To Elaine, my "author buddy," I thank you for your friendship and shared bits of advice. To George, my editorial consultant, and all the helpful people at iUniverse, I am thankful for your professional advice and consultation. And to my best friend Clara, who has been my encourager and confidante, I thank you.

For God, I offer this book as an instrument to be used for His glory. If this story can touch a heart, bring someone to faith, or help someone deal with a caregiving situation, then I have served Him well.